IT'S A LONG ROAD TO COMONDÚ

A·WARDLAW·BOOK

It's a Long Road to Comondú

MEXICAN ADVENTURES SINCE 1928

WRITTEN AND ILLUSTRATED BY *Everett Gee Jackson*

TEXAS A&M UNIVERSITY PRESS : COLLEGE STATION

COPYRIGHT © 1987 BY EVERETT GEE JACKSON

ALL RIGHTS RESERVED

MANUFACTURED IN THE UNITED STATES OF AMERICA

FIRST EDITION

Library of Congress Cataloging-in-Publication Data

Jackson, Everett Gee, 1900–
  It's a long road to Comondú.
  (A Wardlaw book)
    1. Mexico—Description and travel—Anecdotes,
facetiae, satire, etc. 2. Mexico—Social life and
customs—Anecdotes, facetiae, satire, etc.
3. Jackson, Everett Gee, 1900– . I. Title.
II. Series.
F1215.J23 1987   917.2'0482   86-14353
ISBN 0-89096-296-0

TO MY TWO GRANDSONS

Stephen and Winthrop Waterman

CONTENTS

COLOR PLATES

The story of my first four years of painting in Mexico is told in my book *Burros and Paintbrushes: A Mexican Adventure* (Texas A&M University Press, 1985). I also tell in that book how my interest in Mexico may have begun when I took part in a mock Battle of the Alamo staged by my school when I was in the first grade. In that battle I was supposed to be shot by a Mexican, but I never believed he would want to do that to me. Later, during all my years painting in that beautiful and friendly land, I felt that I was searching for this man, and he came to symbolize for me the "spirit of Mexico," which I hoped to capture in my paintings.

I had gone to Mexico from the Art Institute of Chicago in 1923 with Lowell Houser, another art student. At that time, the Mexican Revolution had about simmered down. After we had made drawings and paintings of what we saw in the villages of Chapala and Ajijic, and in Guanajuato, for nearly three years, I returned to the States on a short visit and brought back with me from California my black-haired bride, Eileen.

The three of us moved into El Manglar, a run-down mansion on Lake Chapala formerly used by Mexico's old dictator Porfirio Díaz. Soon heavy rains caused the lake to threaten our house and we moved to Coyoacán, a suburb of Mexico City. After painting there a few months, Lowell, whom the Mexicans called Lowelito, went with archaeologists to work in the Mayan ruins of Yucatán. Eileen and I moved on down to the old Zapotec city of Tehuantepec in the tropics. Three months later in that place, an attack of malaria put a temporary end to our Mexican adventures. A Japanese doctor in Tehuantepec cured me of chills and fevers, but they had so weakened me that he strongly advised us to get out of the tropics.

When we crossed back into the United States in the spring of 1927 my ears were still ringing from quinine, but we both were determined not to let malaria or anything else keep us from returning to Mexico. This book carries on the story of my search, beginning in 1928 and continuing over many years.

PUBLISHER'S ACKNOWLEDGMENT

The Texas A&M University Press is privileged to add its imprint to this Wardlaw Book. The designation claims a special place in the list of Texas A&M publications.

Supported with funds inspired by the initiative of Chester Kerr, former head of Yale University Press, this book, along with its companion volumes, perpetuates the association of Frank H. Wardlaw's name with a select group of titles appropriate to his reputation as man of letters, distinguished publisher, and founder of three university presses.

Donors of these funds represent a wide cross-section of Frank Wardlaw's admirers, including colleagues from scholarly presses throughout the country as well as those from other callings who recognize and applaud the many contributions that he has made to scholarship, literature, and publishing in his four decades of active service.

The Texas A&M University Press acknowledges with profound appreciation these donors.

Mr. Herbert S. Bailey, Jr.
Mr. Robert Barnes
Mr. W. Walker Cowen
Mr. Robert S. Davis
Mr. John Ervin, Jr.
Mr. William D. Fitch
Mr. August Frugé
Mr. David H. Gilbert
Mr. Kenneth Johnson
Mr. Chester Kerr

Mr. Robert T. King
Mr. Carl C. Krueger, Jr.
Mr. John H. Kyle
John and Sara Lindsey
Mrs. S. M. McAshan, Jr.
Mr. Kenneth E. Montague
Mr. Edward J. Mosher
Mrs. Florence Rosengren
Mr. Jack Schulman
Mr. C. B. Smith

Publisher's Acknowledgments

Mr. Richard A. Smith
Mr. Stanley Sommers
Dr. Frank E. Vandiver

Ms. Maud E. Wilcox
Mr. John Williams

Their bounty has assured that Wardlaw Books will be a special source of instruction and entertainment to the reading public for many years to come.

IT'S A LONG ROAD TO COMONDÚ

CHAPTER ONE

Baja California

When Eileen and I crossed the border at Nuevo Laredo, Mexico, into the town of Laredo, Texas, in April, 1927, I saw at once that I had been bewitched. In my own mind there was no doubt about my condition. But I did not learn until later that Mexico had also bewitched Eileen.

The instant we entered the streets of Laredo, in the United States, we saw that everything was clean and orderly. The dirt, so much in evidence in Mexico, was here covered with cement pavement. The sidewalks did not have any holes into which one could easily fall and break his neck. Everything was the way we knew any sane and healthy person would prefer it to be.

Because our arrival in the United States was early in the morning, the first thing we did was go into a little restaurant for breakfast. We had no difficulty choosing what to eat, for all the breakfasts on the menu were numbered. There was number one: "Ham or bacon, eggs — any style — orange juice, toast, and coffee." There was number two: "Hot cakes and maple syrup, orange juice, and coffee." And there was number three: "Cereal, prunes, orange juice, milk, and coffee." When we went into a hotel to wait for our train north, we found that the bathtub, unlike those we had known in Mexico, was not filled with old newspapers and magazines and that it was actually hooked up to hot and cold running water. Clearly we were now in a world where common sense, cleanliness, efficiency, and impeccable order reigned supreme. We had come back to a land where all inconveniences had been eliminated. We had departed from a land in which, in a sense, nothing was in order, a land where the people seemed to be too busy living to have time to straighten things out. But despite this nice new situation, we were not at all happy. We did not prefer this efficiency. Surely we both had been bewitched.

I had lost so much weight that Eileen insisted I needed a rest. After all, the Japanese doctor in Tehuantepec had warned that, because I had malaria, I should take care or I might get tuberculosis. The kind of rest we had in mind, however, was not the kind fate had arranged for me. Almost before we knew it, I had become an instructor at a college in San Diego, California, and Eileen was tied down to a desk writing a social column for a newspaper. We had landed in a groove, but we both knew we were still bewitched. Fate had placed us within a few minutes' drive of the Mexican border, and we began hatching new schemes. There it was, we thought: the same old Mexico we had been forced to leave. We would just go down and cross the border every day, or week, or month we might have off and be right back with our old friend. That is how our life became one long series of trips into Mexico.

We were in for a surprise. The Mexico we would now enter upon crossing the nearby border was Baja California — a land different from the Mexico we had known before. Nevertheless, it was Mexico. The people there spoke Spanish and lived, loosely, under Mexican laws. About all we knew of Baja California beyond that, however, was that it was a long, thin peninsula stretching southward from the California border some eight hundred miles and that it was divided from the Mexican mainland by a narrow strip

of water called by some the Gulf of California, and by others the
Sea of Cortés. We had learned this much from maps, but really
we were ignorant of Baja California geography. We had had no
direct contact with the land or with the people who lived there.
We knew very well, however, that when we started going down
into Baja we would not have studied up and prepared ourselves
beforehand. Lowelito had already changed our attitude toward
the importance of acquiring knowledge of places. Before listening
to him we, like everyone else, believed that the more knowledge
a person had, the better off he would be. Lowelito, however, did
not believe that. He said that a person could be a glutton for
knowledge and that this gluttony could cause a kind of mental
indigestion, doing much harm.

At this point, Lowelito was not with us. He was still in Yucatán
with Jean Charlot and Dr. Sylvanus Morley, but his beliefs about
how an artist should look at the world had changed our own point
of view. Eileen said that if we really were bewitched, it was not
altogether because of Mexico. Lowelito had had a part in it, too.

Lowelito had told us that we might as well face it: artists were
different. The reason they were different was that the world they
lived in was revealed to them only by their sense organs — their
eyes, their ears, their noses, and so on — not by thinking.

Lowelito said that when our minds are full of ideas or knowledge, there is no room for noticing colors, sounds, odors, the shapes
of objects, the way the wind feels on our face, and the way the
ground feels under our feet. He held that there is a sensory world
as well as a world built of thought. He even regarded that sensory
world as a "valuable resource," just as oil, minerals, and lumber
are valuable resources. He believed that the sensory world was
really out there. However, he was sure that most people never got
in touch with it, that because of their insensitivity to it, they usually messed it up. Lowelito never tried to convince us he was right,
but, living around him so long, we began to see the way he did.

When Eileen and I started going to Baja California, we realized
at once that its beauty was explained by the fact that it had not
been "developed." Its beauty was natural beauty. We soon learned
that this natural beauty was still there only because Baja California had practically no natural resources, no lumber, oil, gold, or

silver, nor even much rich land for agriculture. Because it had not been messed up by those who search for natural resources, that "sensory resource" was everywhere you might look.

On our first trip into Baja we went in an old Ford sedan. At that time there were no good roads leading into Baja beyond the town of Ensenada, eighty miles south of the border. When a person left Ensenada to go south, he would have to choose one of the many primitive dirt roads others had made before him. Sometimes these roads, or trails, were fairly close together, scattered only a mile or so apart, but at other places they led off for miles from each other. Eventually, though, they all led south.

Eileen and I had thrown into our car a couple of cots, some cans of water, and what food we would need. Our equipment was spare and primitive. Each day on that trip we would follow one of the trails south of Ensenada until time to stop for the night. Then, wherever we were at that moment, we would camp—right in the middle of the road. I would set up the cots behind the car, and that was where we would sleep. Once, in the middle of the night, another car came along the same trail, but the driver just went around us and kept going south. Eileen didn't even wake up.

One evening, as we were preparing supper, an Indian appeared out of the darkness. We were not at all surprised; in other remote places in Mexico, even around Chapala, a Mexican would often show up suddenly out of nowhere. The Indian who arrived in our camp that night was a native, a *campesino*. Because we were already seated at a folding bridge table with plates on it, Eileen invited him to have supper with us. She had been nursing a pound of butter—four cubes—through the heat, keeping a damp cloth around the butter and letting the wind blow over it. When she had served the food, she took the plate with the four butter cubes on it and said to the *campesino* in Spanish, *"Tome usted mantequilla, por favor."* ("Please take some butter.") Gently and gratefully he accepted her kind offer, but to her surprise he took one whole cube, a quarter of her treasure. And ate it. We hoped it would not give him indigestion.

We learned from him that he had been born and raised in that area and that he had never been north of Ensenada. In a nearby canyon, which we could not see from where we were camped, he

had a small farm, where he raised beans, squash, corn, and tomatoes for his own use. He also had a few goats. But he did not
have a wife. The lack of a wife may have given him a desire to
go away, although I had always thought it was the woman in a
family who longed to go traveling. He told me that he wanted to
ask me an important question but did not want me to answer as
a *norteamericano.* Nor would he ask the question as a Mexican.
"I want our conversation to be purely between two men — *hombre
a hombre* [man to man]," he said. What he wanted to know was
whether or not he could get a job if he took the chance of sneak-
ing illegally across the border into the United States.

I told him that because there were many Mexicans living in Los
Angeles, I felt sure he could find a job if he went there. I said it
would be better to get papers and cross the border legally. I also
told him that in my opinion life was much better in Baja than in
a crowded, noisy city like Los Angeles.

.   .   .

After I brought Eileen home from the hospital with our new
baby girl, in August, 1928, it was months before we even thought
about another trip to Baja California. We had decided to name
our child Jerry, whether it turned out to be a boy or a girl. When
it proved to be a girl, we called her Jerry Gee, adding my middle
name to Jerry, which may have sounded more feminine. Eileen
had made me promise to tell her, the instant the baby arrived,
how it was. She seemed to think it might be some kind of monster. The baby was charming, and the personality she had upon
arrival remained the same thereafter.

Not having a studio, I had set up my easel in a small garage
behind our house, and now I began painting a picture of a Zapotec Indian family, based on my observations before the malaria
struck me in Tehuantepec. The picture was of an Indian man, his
wife, and their first baby. When it was completed, I entered it in
the annual San Francisco Art Association show at the San Francisco Museum of Art. To my complete surprise, the painting was
awarded first prize, along with three hundred dollars. I would
have been content just to have had it accepted in the exhibition.
I tried to figure out why it was given the prize, and decided it was

because I had painted it in such a simple way that it afforded the observer a fresh "seeing experience." This was the second time I had shown a painting in a major American exhibition. The year before, my painting of the charcoal burners, which I had painted while living in Ajijic, had been accepted at the annual American exhibition at the Chicago Art Institute, although it certainly had not won a prize.

Soon we were making other trips into Baja, thanks to the fact that Eileen's parents lived in San Diego and were so happy to take care of Jerry Gee at any time. When we passed the border town of Tijuana and entered the countryside beyond, we were always thankful that God had seen fit not to put a lot of natural resources on that peninsula. In Baja, nature seemed to get along just fine with boojum trees, big and little rocks, palm trees, cacti, desert flowers, sand, wind, heat and cold, mountains, extinct volcanos, valleys, canyons, and the sky above. In addition, there was a wide variety of animals, including rattlesnakes, horned toads, and millions of birds. In that seemingly endless stretch of land, nature had a completely free hand. Every living thing was on its own there. Eileen once commented that in the wild part of Baja there was neither cooperation nor competition, that no plant or animal helped others get along or tried to hold others back. She added that there was no government among the living things — no dictator nor elected leader — and no religion, but that anybody should be able to sense the overall harmony. Obviously every living thing there took part in that harmonious balance. Eileen said she believed that when a person became aware of the harmonious balance among those living things, he developed a burning desire to have it preserved. For her this proved that in such a natural and wild environment there existed something very important for humanity, that no conceivable change resulting from "development" could ever have as much value. Until man discovered what its value was, she said, he should leave it alone. I told her its value was probably that "sensory resource" Lowelito used to tell us about.

Several years passed before Lowelito finished his work in the Mayan ruins of Chichén Itzá. After that, he and a Swedish carpenter, Gustav Stromsvik (who later became a noted archaeologist because of his work in Copán, Honduras), built a boat with their own hands, tore up their tent for sails, and traveled for a year among the islands of the Caribbean Sea. Lowelito made many drawings and block prints of what they were seeing on those islands. Fortunately the college where I taught painting needed a fine printmaker, so I got the president of the college to offer Lowelito the job. He accepted, and soon we were teaching in the same art department. Lowelito then started going with Eileen and me into Baja California. Many times the three of us went down into Baja in the station wagon Eileen and I had recently acquired. On one occasion, though, when Lowelito and I had a week free from our college teaching, Eileen could not get away from her desk at the newspaper, so we reluctantly went without her.

We had met an interesting man in La Jolla, California, and although we knew practically nothing about him, Lowelito asked him if he would like to go along with us.

Not knowing why Lowelito had invited this man, I said, "Lowelito, what made you think this fellow would like to go to the places we go to in Baja?"

"I sized him up," Lowelito answered, "and I decided he was the exact opposite of that philosopher who gave us so much trouble in Chapala." This La Jollan had a beard. We learned that he had shot animals from the back of an elephant in India, and although he talked very little, it was soon obvious that he was, after all, some sort of philosopher himself. Lowelito said, however, that everybody becomes a philosopher the minute he gets some distance below Santo Tomás.

On this trip we went up the canyon where the village of Santo Domingo is located. In the center of that small village is an old ruined Dominican mission, its red adobe walls melted away until they have a smoothness and roundness soothing to look at. We kept on going up the cobblestone street, over which a stream of water flowed the year 'round. We passed through the village and continued to the end of the road. There, across a cornfield, was an adobe house under some large oak trees and enormous fig trees. This turned out to be the home of Señor José Martorel. We called on that gentleman, and, in the shade of the big trees and with a bottle of tequila that Lowelito happened to have in his jacket, we all became lasting friends.

Later that same night, Señor Martorel returned our call. He came on a large mule, which he tethered to a bush near our campfire. The mule was so tall that we had much difficulty getting Señor Martorel up onto its back after Lowelito had served us some of his rum, before and during supper. Because the sand on the road was loose, we had not camped there. Our car was in the road, though. It had got stuck, and we had done what all people do when their cars get stuck: dig under it. So now our car was deep down, as though in a ditch. Even so, we had agreed not to worry, but simply to leave it and have supper. When our guest arrived we did not mention why only the top of our station wagon could be seen from our campfire. Yet I now know that it was Señor Martorel who caused help to arrive the next morning.

We were seated at breakfast when an old sedan drove up. The doors on both sides opened, and people started getting out. There were twelve, and all but the driver were women and children. When they were out, the driver turned off the road, going around our car as though he were on a paved roadway. Soon he returned with a chain, and with his little sedan he pulled our big station wagon up out of the sandy ditch.

At this point the La Jollan said to the driver, "That was very decent of you, old man. Let me reward you for pulling us out of the sand." And he handed the driver a five-dollar bill.

The driver was, of course, a Mexican, but he could speak a little English. "Goddam son of a bitch!" he shouted. "Hell, goddam bastard!" and he threw the bill on the ground. He felt insulted that anyone would think he had pulled our car out of the sand for money. Lowelito, with his unfailing gift of knowing when a drink was in order, saved the situation. We all poured rum into our coffee, and on our next trip, when Eileen was along, this same driver gave us a twelve-pound albacore.

. . .

In Baja California one can get his automobile stuck in a number of ways. There is always the deep sand in the canyons. Near the seashore it is easy to get stuck in a peculiar salty mud, especially around San Quintín Bay. Down below El Rosario we once got stuck by driving onto a bed of native succulents. They were so slick that the tires would not take hold.

A couple of days after we had met Señor Martorel, we got stuck on a slick surface near the ocean, not far from Ensenada. As usual, our companion from La Jolla was eager to help. We had found, however, that his ideas for getting out of such difficulties were never acceptable to the Mexicans. When we got stuck on that wet place near Ensenada, we tried several of his schemes before we decided to go over to a Mexican house to see if the inhabitant had a horse.

We found the Mexican very willing to pull us out of the mud. He did not have a horse, he said, but he was the owner of a strong mule.

"*Señores,*" he said, "I have one of the strongest mules in all Baja California. He can pull your car out all by himself."

The owner of the mule described the fine points of his animal until we were very hopeful. He must have painted a vivid picture in the mind of the La Jollan, who now began to ask the Mexican some questions.

"What is this fine animal's name?"

Lowelito and I knew that he had asked the one question that

would be altogether incomprehensible, for animals in Mexico are not usually given names. It was as if he had asked, "What do you call your house?" Finally, after the La Jollan kept insisting, the Mexican said that he called his strong mule a mule. Then he said, "I call a mule a mule, but my own strong mule, he is at this very moment indisposed."

My first thought was that the La Jollan's question had so annoyed the Mexican that he had decided not to pull us out of the mud after all. But that was not so.

"We shall go see my mule," he continued, "and perhaps you can help me raise him."

We found the mule and he definitely was indisposed. He was standing peacefully at the bottom of a well, where he had fallen when the side of the well had caved in.

"Look, there is my mule," the Mexican said. "You can see that he is strong and in good condition. If you can raise him up, he will be so grateful that he will pull your car out of the mud."

The well was not very deep, but if the mule was ever to get out he would need help. Now the La Jollan advanced what seemed to me a sensible plan for getting the mule out of the well. "We shall dig a trench," he suggested, "which will slant down to the bottom of the well. As we dig, we shall let the dirt fall down with the mule. He will climb on top of the dirt, and then finally he will be able to walk up the trench and out onto level ground."

This plan seemed reasonable to Lowelito and me, but perhaps the Mexican was noting that it had been suggested by the one who had asked, "What do you call your mule?" He would have none of it.

"It is better that we build a *trípode* (tripod) over the well," he said. "Then, with the windlass and a belt of canvas around the mule's belly, we can lift him back into this world."

To erect the tripod and windlass, which we borrowed from a nearby neighbor's well, took so long that we had to camp that night and finish the job the next morning. When we finally got the mule up to where he was swinging and kicking in midair over the well, Lowelito suddenly shouted at us to hold him there until he got his camera. "Nobody will believe this," he shouted, "if we don't have a picture." I thought that was asking a lot, but I could

see his point. The picture was taken, and we managed to swing the mule over to safety. Lowelito then passed the rum bottle around to celebrate our success. Soon after that we all went over to our car, and sure enough, the mule pulled it out of the mud.

We could now say that — on that occasion, at least — we were able to repay a Mexican for doing us a favor. We paid in advance, but there is a subtle difference between handing a man a five-dollar bill and raising his strong mule up out of a well.

.   .   .

On the many trips Eileen and I took into Baja California, we often commented about how different Baja was from the mainland of Mexico. On the mainland we were constantly fascinated by old churches and aqueducts, old haciendas, and even pre-Columbian pyramids and temples — and, of course, by people and donkeys. In Baja California, on the other hand, our attention was held by mountains and valleys, the big sky, beaches and deserts, trees, cacti, rattlesnakes, coyotes, wild burros, and the noticeable scarcity of people. But when I asked Eileen if she felt we were not in Mexico while traveling in Baja, she said that despite the great differences, she definitely felt she was in Mexico. We agreed that there was a distinct, mysterious quality wherever you might be in that country. I remembered seeing a *nopal* cactus once on a high Mexican mountain. It was growing in the snow. That cactus seemed to say that regardless of altitude, the place where it was growing was still Mexico, and therefore it could grow in the snow if it wanted to. This intangible spirit could also be sensed among animals. I have never seen a donkey, or even a dog, outside Mexico that looked Mexican.

Another Mexican characteristic we had sensed was that the people love to live in very small spaces. This trait may be an Indian one, handed down from pre-Spanish times, for it becomes more noticeable among the poor Indian people and those who still live a kind of tribal life. It is a preference for small volumes, at least as far as their shelters are concerned. Eileen believes that this trait may reflect the Indian's reaction to the bigness of the outside world, to which he is so very sensitive. His feeling for the vastness of the sky and the endless stretch of the land may cause him to want a small shelter in which to rest and feel secure.

I remembered those small grass and tule houses I had painted around Chapala, and also the little straw houses across the vacant lot in Mexico City where we used to buy milk. There are many examples of this Mexican preference for small living spaces. Of all the examples of this widespread trait, though, the most impressive we found was an abandoned village on the Pacific Coast side of Baja California, about seventy miles south of Ensenada. This village had been a bustling fishing village down in a secluded draw, or canyon, which was itself like a crack in the endless brush-covered plain. For some reason the people had suddenly abandoned the site and built another village a few miles away, near the main trail south. The houses in this new village were also noticeably small. When Eileen and I went into that canyon leading down to the sea, not a person lived there, not even a dog. The houses were so small that one might have thought the former inhabitants had been a race of pygmies. Some of the rooms were not much larger than filing cabinets.

. . .

All those early roads going south from Ensenada would converge and lead into each little village along the way. Then, after several years, they were replaced by a graded road, straight and built up on an embankment. Finally, but years later, and step by step, the graded road became a paved road, narrow but smooth.

At first it was paved only as far as Arroyo Seco, about a hundred miles below Ensenada. Then, after ten or twelve years, the paved road came alive again, and began to grow longer. It reached Colonia Guerrero, and continued growing past the point where the horrible washboard road turns off to the old mill at San Quintín Bay. In a year or two it had reached El Rosario de Arriba. And it kept on growing. We could never find any workmen making that road. We would go down past the spot where the pavement ended and be gone a week or so, and when we would return the pavement would meet us farther down. But we hardly ever saw workmen.

We had mixed feelings about that growing road. It was a pleasure to ride over its smooth pavement, but we felt depressed over what it might do to the virgin country. Even the Baja natives had misgivings about it. Anita Espinoza, who had run a store in El Rosario for many years, said to us, "Bad road, good people; good road, bad people."

We traveled over all those roads: first, over the dirt ones; later, over the road that was graded and covered with sharp rocks, which produced a bad washboard effect; and eventually, over all the different lengths of pavement. Despite our experience with all those roads, we always knew we could never rest until we had traveled over the one that led to Comondú. Max Miller, who wrote *I Cover the Waterfront,* had worked on a newspaper with Eileen before we were married. Later he had gone to that village with the thought of writing a book about Baja. He told us that it was by far the most interesting place in all the peninsula, and also the most remote and difficult to reach. The people there, he said, were so primitive they didn't even like to accept Mexican pesos. After talking with him, Eileen and I were convinced that some day we would have to visit Comondú, regardless of the condition of the road.

After passing the village of Santo Tomás and climbing out of its beautiful valley, you come before long to where some giant took a great many little white boxes and, standing off at a distance, unloaded them helter-skelter, in one sweeping throw, all over the hills and into the depressions. This is San Vicente. There is absolutely no visible evidence of unity among the little white houses there, and yet the confusion is a visual delight. Perhaps the existence of all those scattered white houses on the bare brown hills is pleasing because of the startling contrast.

When you go below San Vicente, instead of seeing objects scattered here and there, you become more aware of the space in which those objects exist. You actually notice the space itself. And you discover that it is not at all disconnected or broken or fragmented. There are no holes in it; it goes on and on without breaks. It even goes right through objects. But something even stranger happens down there. If you keep on going over those roads, you will eventually find that time has the same characteristics as space. Just as you can look in any direction into space, down there you will do the same with time. You will recall occurrences that took place along those roads years before as readily as those that happened yesterday.

The distance from San Vicente to Colonia Guerrero always seemed endless to us, regardless of which of all those roads through time and space we were traveling over. Colonia Guerrero has an even more elusive order than San Vicente. You will see houses there, but you will never know for sure where the village is. It is easy to go right through the little town without realizing it. In the early days of our traveling in Baja, the roads came into the place from all angles and departed in all directions.

We arrived in Colonia Guerrero quite early one morning, for we had camped only about eight miles from the village. Lowelito, as usual, had pitched his pup tent in front of the station wagon, while Eileen and I had put up our cots directly behind it, so that our entire encampment was strung out along the dirt road for about forty feet. We had a very comfortable camp, but because one of our tires had developed a slow leak, which tended to bother me, we had decided to get up early and go straight to Mr. Gómez's store for breakfast, instead of cooking our own in the roadway.

Mr. Gómez's store and restaurant were open when we got there, and although our breakfast order was taken the minute we sat down at one of the handmade tables, the breakfast was very slow arriving. Eileen said the delay was probably because the cook had gone home the night before without washing all the dishes that had piled up during the day. Her remark did not in the least imply that she was in a hurry. By the time you get as far down even as San Vicente, you lose any tendency to hurry and, from there on south, you like to be wherever you happen to be, at whatever time. In fact, you may need to be reminded of your destination — if you still have one. I had noticed that attitude countless times. I had decided, after thinking about it, that people get that way down in Baja because they start living with nature as a whole, with everything — the mountains, the sky, the space, trees, bushes, and animals of all sorts — and not just with people. Lowelito believed that the natives had no desire for progress because of this attitude. He said that if a person wanted to be a success and make lots of money, he should keep his mind off nature as a whole and stick strictly to the social world of people. He should never think of himself as a part of nature.

The three of us were sitting there having breakfast and talking about such matters when Mr. Gómez came into the restaurant. As usual, it was a pleasure to see him, for he had a way of making you feel that your arrival had made his day.

"*Amigo mío*," he said, after I had told him about our tire trouble, "that slow leak doesn't matter at all. El mecánico, Señor Canon, will fix it very soon. All you need do is drive to his house, on the little hill, and he will fix it very quickly. He also will pump the tire up, because he has a machine to do that work." Mr. Gómez then told us how to find "el mecánico."

After breakfast, following Mr. Gómez's directions, we soon found the house of Señor Eduardo Canon. Despite its simplicity, it stood out from all the other houses, mainly because its landscaping had been done exclusively with deceased automobiles. I remembered a story about a hidden canyon in Africa to which old elephants retire to die. Viewing the yard around the house of Eduardo Canon, we could easily have believed that most of the old automobiles of Baja California had been able to struggle to that place before giving up the ghost. As I looked at all those old wrecks, I had a sinking feeling that perhaps our station wagon might choose to remain there.

As soon as we drove up, Mr. Eduardo Canon came out of his little house. Unlike all the other houses, which were made of adobe, his was made of wood, and it was set upon wooden blocks that raised it off the ground. Eileen was so struck by Mr. Canon's resemblance to the movie actor Wallace Beery that she started whispering to me about it. Mr. Canon could not have overheard her, because Eileen always whispers so faintly that I rarely understand what she has said. But he must have known what she was saying, for he began telling us that he knew where the best hunting was in the area, and that his friend Wallace Beery came down from Hollywood every year to go hunting with him. We were delighted to think of those two out hunting together, looking so much alike.

It amused me to think how strange it would be to any native they might meet who had been of the opinion that there was only one "El Mecánico" in Colonia Guerrero.

After a few minutes children began coming out of Mr. Canon's house. They kept coming out, one at a time, until there were eight. They were all girls, and every one was blond.

"Mr. Canon," Eileen asked, "are all these children yours?"

"Yes, ma'am," he answered, "they are all mine. My wife is inside with the others."

Eileen, being inquisitive, was not slow to enter Mr. Canon's house. There she found Mrs. Canon, a Mexican woman, incapacitated because she had broken her leg. With her were the two youngest members of the family, one an infant—and both of them girls.

Because all ten of Mr. Canon's daughters were blonds, while his wife was rather dark, we asked what his ancestry was. He told us that his father was a Pennsylvania Dutchman who settled in Baja California before he, Eduardo, was born. He also told us that his father was buried not far from the Canon house, on a bare hillside where on some nights the coyotes howled, and where wind and rain sometimes made the place very dreary. Marking his father's grave was a simple wooden cross.

By the time Mr. Canon had fixed the slow leak in our tire, Eileen was so charmed by the Canon family that Lowelito was moved to bring out a bottle of rum. After the bottle had been passed around a number of times, our friendship grew so rapidly that Mr. Canon would allow us to pay him for fixing the tire only after much urging, and in turn he was now insisting that we accept a gift from him. The gift turned out to be several large, very heavy boulders of onyx, which he had brought up from a mine below El Rosario. Although our car was already overloaded, there was nothing to do but accept his gift. We had already accepted another gift, in a similar circumstance, which from Eileen's point of view was useless, and which stuck out several feet behind our car. It was one of the longer ribs of a whale. Despite the fact that our car was sagging, Lowelito continued to pass the rum. The thought came to me that this practice of rock-giving might explain all those deceased automobiles around Mr. Canon's house. I went over and looked inside some of them to see if by chance they might be filled with onyx boulders.

Mr. Canon now called all his daughters to one side in a whispered conference, and we were fearful that they might be about to give us some other heavy object. Then Mr. Canon announced that he would like to show us something important. Whatever it was, we knew that we were about to be honored by the entire family.

Mr. Canon motioned us into the house. Although the line of girls and visitors was so long that some of us could not squeeze into the house, Eileen and I did. There we saw Mr. Canon under the bed so far that only his feet were visible. The mystery of his behavior was heightened by the seriousness of all the daughters, who now watched in silence.

Presently Mr. Canon came out, bringing with him something rolled up in a blanket. We all gathered around him as he began to unwrap the package. The first blanket was taken off, then another, then several layers of rags, until finally we beheld an object of wonder. It even seemed to give off a bright light. Actually, the light must have been caused by the high degree of polish, for what we saw was an exquisitely finished cross of white onyx. Carved out of the same kind of rock that Mr. Canon had given us, it was about two feet long.

Mr. Canon had had the cross carved to provide a durable monument for his father's grave, on that lonely hillside. But after it was placed up there, the rains started falling, and the whole family began to worry about the little cross out in the rain and loneliness. It would get stained and spattered with mud, so they decided to bring it back to the house, where it would be protected. As we admired it, we knew that having it there under the bed, wrapped in blankets and rags, must have been a unifying family force, that all those daughters would go through life with a deep feeling of being sisters because of it.

.   .   .

Eileen and I liked to camp on the peninsula that encloses San Quintín Bay. It is a long, narrow stretch of sand dunes, with the bay on the east side and the Pacific Ocean on the west. Several volcanic cones are located about halfway down, and here and there are outcroppings of volcanic rock. Because the road into that place is over the dunes, for many years very few people entered the area. But the deep sand never did keep us out, although sometimes we would get stuck and have to let air out of our tires to get through the sand. Neither did the bad road discourage those Mexicans who dived for sargasso, a kind of seaweed that, we were told, they baled and sold to Japan, where it was made into soup. Nor did the sand keep the lobster fishermen out. But the people in both those industries were few, only three or four families. The houses of the lobster fishermen were thrown together out of driftwood and canvas; those of the sargasso divers were little more than windbreaks made of volcanic rocks piled to form walls about four feet high. Despite these scattered settlements, that whole peninsula was as lonely a place as one could find, especially during the season of fogs.

Normally the air there is fresh and clean. There is no large-scale agriculture, and no insecticides are washed into the ocean — insecticides that cause pelican eggs to become so thin that they break. Consequently many pelicans and thousands of other sea birds live in that area. Once, however, Eileen and I had to choose a campsite that depended entirely on the direction the wind was blowing, for a great gray whale had died out to sea, and the waves had washed it ashore on the long white beach. Smelling a rotting whale is not an enviable experience. The odor is so heavy it seems a wonder that it can be carried by the wind. It is a melancholy odor, in addition to being unbearably offensive, and when it reaches the nostrils you know at once that you are going to leave. Fortunately we were able to find a nearby place that was completely free of the odor. We lingered only two days, since we dared not walk about and run the risk of encountering that unearthly chemical effect. To our surprise, a family of sargasso divers living downwind from the carcass gave no sign of moving camp. When we departed, we waved good-bye to them from a distance.

Some time later we were again in that area. Curious about the condition of the whale, we went back down that sandy strip. When we came to the sargasso camp, the Mexicans were still there. They

invited us in to visit behind their stone windbreaks, and they of-
fered us seats on their newly acquired chairs, which were the up-
turned vertebrae of the dead whale. Its odor had gone away, and
when we visited its remains we found them as white as snow. The
bones had been picked clean by the birds. The long ribs of the
whale were scattered about as though coyotes might have joined
the feast.

Because we were going to drive directly back to the border, Eileen gathered together the food we had left over and took it to
the lobster camp. In giving it to the people there, she was careful to explain that we were going across the border, where the
officials would not let us take the food. It is important to use the
same tact in making gifts down there as in receiving them.

Early the next morning, we were packed and ready to leave
when two lobster fishermen suddenly appeared out of a dense fog.
The fog made them look like two dark gray giants. Each man held
aloft two of the biggest *langostas* (lobsters) I had ever seen. They
must have been over two feet long. As the men held them out
toward us, one man said, with a happy smile on his face, *"Quere-
mos darles unas langostas de regalito."* ("We want to give you a
little present of lobsters.")

We knew we could not accept those lobsters. We had no way
to keep them or get them across the border. But to decline would
be difficult. I was wishing that Lowelito were present; he would
know how to handle the situation. He would have broken out a
bottle of rum, and in the end we not only would have accepted
the big lobsters but would have stayed over until we had boiled
and eaten them.

I had to thank the lobster fishermen and try to explain why we
could not accept what they called a *regalito* (little gift). The de-
jected look on their faces as they stood there holding out those
squirming lobsters in the gray fog made us so sad that we almost
decided to do what Lowelito would surely have done.

.   .   .

The many trips Eileen and I were taking down into the primitive part of Baja California were making me almost exclusively
a landscape painter. But I was still interested in figure composi-

tion. Consequently, during the 1930s, when I noticed that the
only people in San Diego who seemed to be set apart from the
general population were sailors on shore leave, I painted several
of them.

One day Jerry Gee walked into my studio wearing a brand-new
hat Eileen had bought her. She also had on blue socks and a blue
dress. She was so charming that I asked her if she would pose for
me. To my surprise she not only was willing, but she held as still
as a stone while I painted her portrait. My only interest was to
make that portrait as much "like" her as possible. Jerry Gee was
seven years old.

. . .

After Lowelito, the La Jollan, and I had been pulled out of the
sand in Santo Domingo Canyon, on that early trip to Baja, we
had gone with José Martorel to salute his father, who lived at the
edge of the village. Don José had told us that his father was the
keeper of all the old church statues that had been in the Santo
Domingo Mission many years before. When the old mission roof
had fallen in and the walls had begun to melt away, something
had to be done with the numerous saints and Virgins, so Don
José's father had taken them into his place.

His house was very picturesque. Made of weatherworn adobe
brick, it had a red tile roof. On one side, connected to the house,
was a *ramada* (a shedlike room, open on three sides), over which
a large grapevine had grown. Don José Martorel was then in his
late sixties; his father must have been in his late eighties. The old
man's hair was snow white, and he looked very dried up, but he
was agile. He invited us into his house, and when Don José told
him we would like to see the *figuras religiosas* (religious figures),
he led us into an adjoining room with a dirt floor. Standing on
the floor of this room, all along the walls, were the saints and
Virgins. The floor itself was covered from wall to wall with very
large pumpkins and some squashes of a kind called "cushaw" in
east Texas.

About ten years later, Eileen and I were passing through Colonia Guerrero on our way to the border. It occurred to me that
Eileen might like to see the house where José Martorel's father had

lived. I assumed that the old man would no longer be alive; for he would have been close to a hundred years old. Don José had been killed in an automobile accident several years before — ironic, because he rarely rode in an automobile. We turned off the road at Colonia Guerrero and continued on up Santo Domingo Canyon toward the village. On entering the village of Santo Domingo, I turned to the left, to where the old man's house had stood.

I said to Eileen, "If the house is still there, maybe the old church figures will still be in it. I surely would like you to see them."

The house was just as I had remembered it. Nor did it look abandoned. A dog came running out wagging his tail instead of barking at us. The dirt yard had been swept clean with a brush broom, which was leaning against the front wall of the house. A scrawny chicken, almost completely devoid of feathers, was walking about the yard as if it owned the place, and growing out of the dry dirt was a rose vine whose bright pink roses were scattered along a low wooden fence. Everything was quiet.

I walked up to the front door and knocked. Then I thought I had better speak out, so I shouted, "*Señor o señora ¿hay gente en esta casa?*" ("Sir or madam, are there any people in this house?")

I thought I could hear a noise inside, and then the door opened. Out stepped a little old white-headed man in a pale blue shirt. He looked very much like the old man I had met there years before. However, I knew that could hardly be possible, so I spoke to him cautiously.

"Señor," I said, "pardon me, but I came here many years ago with Don José Martorel and met his father, who was then guarding the *figuras religiosas*. I thought those figures might still be here and that I might see them again. My name is Everardo Jackson, and this is my wife."

The little old man stood very still for a moment, with his hands held close to his chest. Then he looked up at me and seemed to be studying my face. Finally he began to smile.

In a squeaky voice, he said, "*El tiempo no existe. Solamente existe la vida, como Dios quiere. Soy el papá de José. He vivido en este cañón por muchos años, pero Dios me ha olvidado.*" ("Time does not exist. Only life exists, as God wills it to exist. I am José's father. I have lived in this canyon for many years, but God has forgotten me.")

He added that one of these days God was going to say to Himself, "Oh, I have forgotten old Martorel, up that Santo Domingo Canyon. He has been there long enough, so I will now call him in."

The old man did not say that he remembered me, but he graciously invited us into his house and led us into the room where the saints and Virgins were still standing against the walls. Only a few cushaws were on the dirt floor, which made it easier to examine the religious figures.

CHAPTER TWO

Return to Chapala

By the year 1950, Eileen and I had made so many trips into Baja California that we had lost count of them, but over all those years we had not been able to get back to the mainland of Mexico. We had seen our little girl, Jerry Gee, grow up. Now she was a student at Stanford University. During all this time we knew that Mexico had bewitched us, that sooner or later we would have to go back to Chapala, to Mexico City, and even to Tehuantepec.

When the first opportunity came, however, it did not include Eileen. The dean of the college where I was teaching called me into his office and asked if I would introduce a course on the history of Middle American art. I told him that I would love to teach such a course if I could have a year to prepare the materials for it. I would need to visit some Mexican museums and several archaeological sites before I would feel capable of lecturing on that subject. When the summer vacation period arrived, Eileen could not get away from her newspaper column. Lowelito, on the other hand, whose vacation came at the same time as my own, was free to accompany me. He was also glad to come along, especially since he had worked about five years in the Mayan ruins of Yucatán and wanted to become better acquainted with the ancient art of other parts of Mexico.

I now remembered what Eileen had said to me when we crossed back into the United States twenty-three years before: "You will return to Mexico, but don't forget, I will be with you when you do." So it was with a heavy heart that I left her behind. I was determined that this would be only one of many trips, and that in the future she would be with me.

Lowelito and I departed for southern Mexico. This trip would take us all the way to the old Mayan city of Palenque. But we decided to stop off in Chapala to see our old Mexican friends Alfredo Padilla and Isidoro Pulido before continuing on south.

.   .   .

I had always believed that I myself never changed, even though my body grew older, my eyes weaker, my hearing more faint, and my hair streaked with white. When Lowelito and I arrived this time in Chapala, we found that Alfredo had become stockier and slightly bowlegged, while Isidoro was now a grown man whose waistline had almost doubled. But it did not take long for us to discover that they themselves were the same — our old and loyal friends. The changes we noticed in their appearance had nothing whatever to do with themselves, and almost immediately we ceased to be aware of those changes. I could not help wondering if the memory I had of their youthful appearance would not be obliterated and replaced by the way they appeared today.

Isidoro had become a maker of candy and a dealer in pre-Columbian art in the patio of his house on Los Niños Héroes Street. I did not teach him to make candy, but when he was just a boy I had shown him how he could reproduce those figurines he and Eileen used to dig up back of Chapala. Now he not only made them well, but he would also take them out into the fields and gullies, bury them, and then dig them up in the company of American tourists, who were beginning to come to Chapala in increasing numbers. Isidoro did not feel guilty when the tourists bought his works; he believed his creations were just as good as the pre-Columbian ones.

Alfredo, who had owned a little drugstore when we were living in El Manglar, had closed it in 1927 and joined the Cristero Revolution. He was now a carpenter specializing in coffins.

On the first night of our 1950 visit, Lowelito and I went to Isidoro's house. Isidoro had set up a dining table under the *ramada* that faced the patio where he made his candy and pre-Columbian figures. As I watched him mix drinks for us, I kept saying to myself, "Isidoro is the same. He is no longer a slim youth; he now has a wife who is about to serve us a Mexican dinner, and he has several children. But he is the same." I was thinking similar thoughts about Alfredo.

Isidoro handed each of us a tall glass of his cold drink as we seated ourselves around the table. Behind us was a white plaster wall, which reflected the dim light of a kerosene lamp. At one end of the *ramada*, another table was littered with broken pottery, ancient clay figurines — probably models for Isidoro's fakes — and five human skulls he had dug up when he had found the figurines. After I had taken several sips of Isidoro's drink, the skulls seemed to be looking at us and listening to everything we were saying. Lowelito commented that the skulls were very expressive, that each one was as singular as its living head must have been. I could certainly see that each skull did have its own distinct personality, and for the first time I became aware of the connection between the bony structure of a person's head and the expression on his face. I had always assumed that facial expressions were caused solely by muscle and skin action. Now it occurred to me that the expressions on a face are simply variations on the expression of the skull itself.

Isidoro's drink, which was mixed with fruit juice, did not taste alcoholic but must have been potent. Alfredo was now staring at those skulls as though he had just seen a ghost. Suddenly he began to talk about them, but not to anyone in particular. He seemed rather to be talking out loud to himself. He spoke in English, but in his Mexican way. It was a style he had acquired because of having learned English from a dictionary.

"I don't like those skulls," he said. "I don't like to sit here with those people. They are like that up-and-down monster I once saw when I was coming from Ixtlaoacán in the night. As I crossed a little brook, that monster came splashing along up the brook. I believe it was one of those fellows. They do not like me!"

As we sat silently, thinking of this strange story of Alfredo's, Isidoro's son, Remigio, came into the light from the dark kitchen doorway behind us and began to spray something onto a procession of ants going up the limb of a tree in the patio. All those ants were carrying little green leaves, which made them look like a row of miniature sailboats.

Now Isidoro spoke, in Spanish. He could understand a little English, but he could not speak it. "That is like the time I was coming one night from Jocotepec. I was coming this side of Ajijic and there was a moon over San Miguel. Then I looked ahead, and in the road was a fantastic animal. '¡Ay! ¡Qué caray!' I said. 'What an animal! What a devil!' It was like a big devilfish with five bodies. But when I threw a rock at it, it broke apart into five animals, for it was those burros of Carlos and they all had their heads together like a wheel."

We sat around talking about our early days in Chapala until late in the night. Then we went out into the streets, which were dark as only Mexican streets can be. Isidoro and Alfredo walked with us to our hotel and waited with us outside until the *mozo* unbolted the door.

. . .

The hotel we were now in was not the Mólgora Hotel, which we had known in the twenties. The Mólgora had long since ceased to exist, except as a ruin. We were now staying in the Hotel Nido, which was behind the old Mólgora. The word *nido* means "nest," but it also was the name of the lady who owned the hotel. The Nido was a pleasant, colonial-type hotel, but the contrast with the old Mólgora Hotel was quite shocking. Like Isidoro's girth and Alfredo's bowed legs, it symbolized the changes that had been taking place all over Mexico, and perhaps all over the world.

When Lowelito and I went down to breakfast the next morning, we found Isidoro and Alfredo waiting for us in the lobby. They had eaten already, but they sat with us. I now asked Alfredo if the ancient pyramid I had noticed years ago on the road between Ajijic and Jocotepec was still the way it was when we were living in Ajijic. It was then a mound of earth in a cornfield on the lake side of the road, not very far below Ajijic. Obviously it was the remains of a pyramid built by the Indians before the arrival of the Spanish conquerors.

"Would that land be for sale?" I asked Alfredo. "I might want to buy it and build a retirement house on it."

"We shall go and inquire tomorrow," said Alfredo. "We shall go to that pyramid of our ancestors. We shall go and take a lunch. You, Isidoro, will prepare a delicious lunch with cucumbers. We go in the morning, on the *camión* (bus)."

After breakfast, we walked out to the end of the *muelle* (pier) and then up past the old railroad station, which was now abandoned. Soon we came to a group of little straw houses beneath some willow trees right at the edge of the lake. I remembered painting a picture of those same houses in 1923, when Lowelito and I were living in Chapala in the House with the Green Door. Like the railroad station, the straw houses were abandoned. We could see why. Obviously the lake water had almost submerged them at times over the years. The trunks of the willow trees next to the houses had continued growing, and now they were very large and black. The water of the rising lake had made the trees flourish. I saw that the tender yellow green of their foliage was the same as it had been when I painted them some twenty-seven years before.

That evening we went back along the lakeshore and arrived at the Widow's Place for drinks. As we entered her large restaurant and beer garden near the shore, I was surprised at the reception she gave me. She greeted me as an old friend, although I had known her but slightly, as the wife of Mr. Sánchez, the village photographer. Alfredo told me that because of the drink she had introduced all over Mexico and even into the United States, she was now quite wealthy and famous. It was a nonalcoholic drink, very good as a soothing chaser for tequila. It even worked with bad tequila, the kind Lowelito said had "crotin oil" in it. The drink was called *Sangrita de la Viuda Sánchez*, which Lowelito translated as "the Precious Blood of the Widow Sánchez." Isidoro used to make that same drink for us, and Alfredo told us that Isidoro

had shown the Widow how to make it. She took full advantage of this knowledge, putting the drink on the market. Several years before, Lowelito and I had found the Widow's *Sangrita* for sale in Tijuana, but at that time we had no idea that the Widow Sánchez of the drink's name was the same Mrs. Sánchez we had known in Chapala. In fact, we did not know she had become a widow. I now asked Alfredo what was wrong with Mr. Sánchez that caused him to die and leave his wife a widow.

"Mr. Sánchez died of a sickness," Alfredo answered.

I did not ask him for further details. He had just told me that recently a dead woman had been found on the Isla Alacrán, just off Chapala, and that she had thirty-seven stab wounds in her body. The authorities, he said, concluded that she had committed suicide.

While we were seated at a table in the Widow's Place, a waiter came to us and said there was a man outside who was looking for Señor Jackson. I told him I was Señor Jackson and asked that he show the man to our table. I had no idea who could be looking for me; I had been away from Chapala many years.

Soon I saw the waiter returning with a well-dressed man at his side. He seemed to me to be a "mestizo type," and I did not recognize him. When he approached our table, he came directly to me.

"Ah, señor," he said, "it gives me much pleasure to see you again, and to remember those pretty days when we were so happy living at El Manglar. Do you remember the snake I found under your bed, and how I tried for hours to beat the life out of that snake? The tip of its tail would continue to wiggle, and I would keep beating on it, until it was like *masa*. I think that was one of the most fascinating experiments of my youth!"

I could hardly believe what I was seeing and hearing. This was surely Pancho, the son of Margarita, our cook at El Manglar. We had always thought he was a half-wit. Now it was quite obvious that he was intelligent and looked distinguished.

When Pancho had gone, I said to Lowelito, "I guess you were right when you used to say that down here one never can tell who is stupid and who is not." But Lowelito said that something had happened to Pancho, something had popped loose all of a sudden in his head.

We did not stay long at the Widow's Place, for we wanted to get up early the next morning and go on a bus to the ancient pyramid.

.   .   .

Isidoro met us in the hotel lobby early the next morning. He had a large grass bag over one arm and a quart bottle of gin in one hand. This, it appeared, was going to be a fine day. But when Alfredo arrived, he obviously was troubled.

"My friends," he began, "this is a day of sorrow for me. I cannot go with you. Because of that man and his coffin I must not go. He has been following me again, and I must not go with my dear companions to the pyramid of our ancestors."

We understood what he meant. Upon our arrival in Chapala, Alfredo had closed his carpenter shop for a holiday, which was to last as long as we remained. Unfortunately, though, he was the only coffin maker in the village, and when he closed his shop he left unfinished a coffin for which there was a pressing need. Mr. Rodríguez had said, "The business of the coffin must be terminated!"

As the four of us walked out of the hotel together, Alfredo continued, "I must remain behind and finish that coffin for Señor Rodríguez. He is right when he says that some things can wait only so long. I must not go with you on this picnic."

When we got to the *camión*, we found it already full of people. And more people were climbing into it, loaded with all kinds of belongings, including chickens with their feet tied together. Lowelito and I assured Alfredo that he should not neglect his duty. We told him that soon we would go again to the pyramid. But the look of sadness on his face was ruining the start of our journey.

Suddenly the *camión* engine started. The bus shivered, and the foul odor of gasoline fumes filled the air. This excited the passengers, and it must have set off something in Alfredo. As Lowelito, Isidoro, and I climbed aboard, he exclaimed, "I shall go! I shall go with you to the pyramid! How could you find the owners without me?"

The bus started down Calle Hidalgo, which led into the road to Ajijic and Jocotepec. Soon I was passing places I had known so intimately before. The long interval, far from dimming my memory of them, now seemed to have made those places more meaningful to me. We passed the House with the Green Door, where Lowelito and I had lived in 1923, and a short distance beyond I saw the very spot where I had been sitting at my easel when the Russian woman almost ran over me with her horse. We passed the village of San Antonio, where I could see the churchyard in which two drunken Indians had once struggled playfully with a large pistol, while its bullets churned up the dust among the people. By this time Alfredo apparently had forgotten the coffin. He was talking and laughing as he sat beside Lowelito.

"There was an old lady in Chapala who invited me to marry

with her," he was saying. "And I said to her, 'What are your conditions?' Do you not think I was wise?

"That old woman would enjoy to put me in a cage. She would hang the cage, with me inside it, to her doorway, where I should sing. But I cannot sing in a cage.

"Isidoro! Why do you not mix us a drink? Is this the Widow's Place, which is closing all the time we are getting drunk? Come here, Isidoro, with the bottle!

"Lowelito, do you remember that night of the murder in the street, when it was raining and the old women came with candles under their umbrellas?"

By now, we were bumping through the main street of Ajijic.

There on the right-hand side was our home of those earlier years, just as though we had been away only for a day. But the store was no longer next door. It had been moved across the street and had become the place where the bus stopped.

Ajijic seemed to me to be almost the same, and so did the road leading to it along the lakeshore. It was still a dirt road. Apparently twenty-four years had not been long enough to cause any noticeable changes. Then suddenly I saw someone who made me realize that the years had brought about some changes after all. An old woman, wrapped in a gray *rebozo* (shawl) and covered with dust, was waving frantically at me outside the bus window. The last time I had seen her, she had been a young girl. But she still looked as dirty as the pigs of Chapala and Ajijic.

"Lowelito! Look!" I shouted. "There is La Muda, the deaf-mute!" She had recognized us, and I had recognized her, despite the fact that she now appeared so much older.

Because traveling by Mexican bus is so much faster than donkey-back travel, we might not have noticed the place where Lowelito once met the huge herd of donkeys had it not been for a perfect reminder: Right at that very spot in the lane our bus encountered another herd of burros. As the bus slowed down and began creeping along through the herd, I got Lowelito's attention and pointed at the donkeys on both sides and in front of the bus. Lowelito was seated with Alfredo near the entrance of the bus, and the way he began to laugh assured me that he was living again his wild ride of twenty-four years before. When finally the bus had cleared the herd of burros without any mishap, I noticed that the beautiful lane, bordered on each side with rock fences, had not changed at all. Even the cloud shadows on the dirt road were moving along slowly in the direction of Jocotepec, just as they had moved on that distant day.

A mile or so farther on, we reached a cemetery, which was on the right-hand side of the dirt road. The little wooden crosses decorated with colorful paper flowers created a strange effect there, surrounded by the dry, uncultivated fields. I recalled those times when I had painted pictures in an old abandoned Spanish cemetery in Guadalajara, and now I wished I could make a painting of this little cemetery of the poor peasants of this area.

Two miles farther down the road, Isidoro signaled the bus driver and we were let off in the lane that leads on to Jocotepec. The people remaining in the bus may have been puzzled as the four of us stood there by the side of the road, no village and no house in sight. All along the lane here were large *guaje* trees, and over the rock fence we could see row after row of papaya trees extending down toward the lake.

"Now let us go to the pyramid," said Alfredo, "and drink to the health of our ancestors."

We all climbed over the rock fence into a field of tomato plants from which the tomatoes had recently been harvested. This field was divided from the next by a barbed-wire fence. Following a trail along this fence toward the lake, we soon arrived at the base of the pyramid, which was not more than three hundred yards from the road. The fence continued on up the pyramid and down its other side, cutting it squarely in two. Another fence, running perpendicular to the first one, also went over the top of the pyramid. Thus the pyramid was divided into four equal parts, each enclosed in a different field. But unlike the four fields in which it was standing, the pyramid itself was not cultivated. It was in a wild state, covered with bushes, weeds, trees, and bright red flowers. In fact, it did not look much like a pyramid, but more like a steep mound.

The summit of this pyramid was only about thirty feet above the floor of the surrounding fields. It was not large, but it was a pyramid, and it had been built in pre-Columbian times by those Indians whom the Aztecs were never able to conquer.

Perhaps it was my continued interest in the pre-Spanish civilizations of Mexico that had led the dean of my college to suggest that I offer a course in that subject. And now, with my old Mexican friends, I would be able to examine an ancient pyramid of the type built in western Mexico. I would also be able to look at some of the original figurines Isidoro had collected. I knew he would never try to fool me with any of his fakes.

The people who lived around Lake Chapala before the arrival of the Spanish conquerors created thousands of little baked clay figurines. Many of these figurines — or *monos*, as the natives call them — must have been portraits, for they resemble some of the people who live in the area today. I intended to learn as much as I could about the significance of these figurines, and about the space order they contained, which should reveal the mode of spatial perception of those ancient artists, the way their attention moved over and around objects.

Realizing that the pyramids of western Mexico, unlike most of those in the rest of the country, had been used as tombs, I felt quite certain that the one we were now visiting concealed somewhere within itself the remains of an ancient chief, along with the usual objects that accompanied him to the grave. I was still more certain of this after Isidoro informed me that he had never dug into this pyramid.

"Why have you never searched here for *monos*," I asked him, "when it is so near your house?"

"I have never searched in this pyramid because I could not get a permit," he answered. "Every year, that drunken one, Ignacio Hernández, would grow his corn all the way to the top of it, and he would never allow me to dig into it. This is the first time he has not planted his corn here."

From this it was obvious that, as Isidoro saw the matter, archaeological permits to excavate ancient pyramids were to be had locally, and not from the government.

"Now we must find the owner of the pyramid," I remarked.

"Now we must drink to our coming to the pyramid and to the health of our ancestors," Alfredo corrected me.

Sitting there in the sunshine at the base of that ruin, Isidoro mixed us a drink. We saw him put into it some gin and some lime juice. But he must have added another ingredient when we were not looking, because after I had taken two sips the pyramid became much larger and much grander, and it appeared to be clothed with a mysterious forest. As I looked up at its summit, which now seemed to be shrouded in clouds, I thought I could dimly make out a fantastic castle.

The drink must have had a similar effect on Alfredo. Gazing seriously down into his glass, he began to deplore his drinking habits.

"I do not know in which way I would be able to get rid of this bad habit," he was saying. "Perhaps the only way is to go to a monastery and become a monk. Now that we are older, we understand that wine is the source of many of our troubles. It has produced in me the piles, nervous weakness, and inflammation of the bilious gall. And the more I hate it, the more I often drink.

"But," he added, "this wine we have here is different, and this day is different. With my old friends I now drink this product of Isidoro's to the ancient ones!"

Out of the surrounding space, Indians began to gather, one of them riding a gigantic ox. They accepted some of Isidoro's drink and became a part of our picnic.

"We shall now drink to the health of our ancestors," Alfredo was saying again. "For this peak at whose base we sit is a manmade mountain, raised by the great strength of our ancestors. We owe it to them to drink to their health."

Our newly arrived Indian companions, who, being country people, were of a more serious nature than Alfredo, were struck by the nobility of this sentiment, so the toast that we all drank was a grave and reverent one.

Apparently the presence of two white *gringos* who were drinking to the Indian ancestors made the toast need some clarification, for one of the gentle farmers now asked Alfredo, "To whose ancestors are we drinking this mixture? Those noble ancestors to whose health we drink were *indios*, were they not? They were not *europeos*."

"That is true, Ramón," Alfredo replied. "That is very true, and I know well what you are thinking. But you must remember that among the ancient Indians there was one who was white. He was called Quetzalcoatl. Who knows but that these European friends who drink with us now may be the children of that Quetzalcoatl. That one there with the high shoes, as you can observe for yourself, has a head which is formed like those *ídolos* of Isidoro's."

He was referring to Lowelito, and for the first time I noticed that Lowelito's profile sloped back like that of the ancient Maya, whose heads were elongated artificially at infancy.

"I was thinking," added another of our companions, "how our ancestors, even those of the *europeos*, all came from Father Adán. It is just that some went into one part of the world, while others traveled to different places. So it can be said in truth that we all are now celebrating our ancestors, even though some of us here are *gringos."*

It was in this way that Lowelito and I seemed to have acquired an Indian heritage, and I must admit that on that day, as never before, we felt like Indians.

On one side of the pyramid was a field of *chayotes.* The vines of that strange vegetable made a solid roof over the field, a roof held up by poles. And now from underneath that roof emerged the two uncles of Ramón, wearing their white *calzones* (trousers) rolled up above their knees. They were, however, the uncles of a Ramón of Guadalajara and no kin to the Ramón who had questioned our ancestry. Nevertheless, they were uncles of the Ramón who was the owner of that field and of one-fourth of the pyramid. It seemed that Ignacio Hernández, whom Isidoro had referred to as the drunkard, was the only person living in the area who owned a part of the pyramid, and it became clear that the ownership of the total pyramid, situated as it was in the corners of four fields, was a business involving many different families.

"I think our ancestors had in mind to play a joke," said Ignacio, "when they so cunningly placed this pyramid on the land of so many people." He went on to say that some of the owners were now working on the railroad tracks in Chicago.

The problem of title had become so complex that Alfredo thought more drinks would be needed to work it out. Fortunately, Isidoro had an emergency supply of his ingredients in the bag, and therefore it was not necessary to send the Indian on the spotted ox back to Ajijic.

When it became clear to Alfredo that Lowelito and I could not purchase the pyramid, he thought of a possible alternative.

"Do you remember the cemetery?" he asked. "There is some land for sale right next to that cemetery, and from it there is a fine view of the beautiful paper flowers and crosses."

But the most touching suggestion was that of Ignacio: "As for my one-fourth of the pyramid, it is yours to sit on and get drunk on whenever you wish."

We took leave of our new Indian friends and departed from what had become a magnificent and sacred ruin. The business conference was adjourned, although some Indian members of the board were by now sleeping on the slopes of the pyramid. Their sleep must have been brought on by Isidoro's drink; it was not yet the siesta hour.

It was our intention to get back to the road in time to catch the bus on its return from Jocotepec, but just as we arrived there, a sand truck came by whose driver asked if we cared to ride with him. We were pleased at this opportunity. Lowelito climbed inside the cab, and the rest of us climbed onto the sand. Soon we arrived back in Ajijic. Three of us, however, were covered with sand: Isidoro, Alfredo, and I had dug ourselves down into it to avoid being scraped off by the low limbs of the *guaje* trees.

The Korean War had been going on but a few months. As we now sat in the store, which was also the Ajijic bus station, we were surprised at how the people of Ajijic were taking an interest in that war. They all regarded the Communists as their enemies and considered our war their own. They regarded Communism as the greatest foe both of the Church and the Pope and of their freedom.

As we were enjoying a bottle of beer in the Ajijic store, Alfredo said there could be no better way to round out our lives than to go and kill some Communists. Lowelito and I were certain we had never killed anybody, but we could not be sure about Alfredo, since he had been in a revolution. Of course most Mexican men his age had been in revolutions. That did not necessarily mean that they had killed anybody—or at least that they had killed anybody on purpose. After all, Alfredo had told us several times that he had "the heart of a lamb."

"We should go to Korea on those mules and fight Communists," Alfredo was now saying, for at that moment a herd of little black mules was passing in the cobblestone street. Isidoro took no interest whatever in this suggestion. Communists were to him as meaningless as Korea.

Thinking of mules, I remembered a story told me by a friend who had been in charge of a silver mine up near Zacatecas, where a horrible battle was fought in 1914. I now told Alfredo this story.

Pancho Villa had ridden up to the mine of my friend and demanded all the mules. My friend said to this bandit-general, "This is an English-owned mine. You have no quarrel with the English government and therefore should not take the mules. It is the United States government that has been causing you trouble."

Pancho, according to my friend, reflected upon this information a moment or two. "You are correct," he said; "the English government and I are friends. I should not take anything that belongs to that friendly country. But," he continued, "you must know that the mules are Mexican citizens, and therefore I demand only the mules. They must come and help me fight for our country's freedom."

"I regard all Mexican mules as Mexican citizens myself," said Alfredo. "They have always been good Mexican soldiers."

When the bus from Jocotepec stopped at the Ajijic store, we boarded it immediately and in a very short time arrived back in Chapala. We had been gone only one day, although it seemed to me that we had been away a month. As we stepped off the bus in the blazing red light of late afternoon, there was Mr. Rodríguez waiting for us. The anxious look on his face made me realize that we should never have allowed Alfredo to go with us and neglect finishing the coffin he had promised.

Obviously Mr. Rodríguez was upset, and because Alfredo was slow in reassuring him, I spoke up.

"Señor Rodríguez, I hope this delay with the coffin has not caused you undue alarm. It has been Alfredo's intention all along to get right to work on that job of yours, but he was called away by some business regarding a pyramid. Now we are all going to help him finish the coffin."

We all started walking in the direction of Alfredo's workshop. There were now six of us, Mr. Rodríguez having brought along an Indian *cargador* to carry away the finished coffin. I felt certain that the work would soon be done, for Alfredo had told me he had almost completed the job before we went to the pyramid. But after we had gone about two blocks we came to a cantina along the street, and, to my alarm, Alfredo turned and went right through its swinging half-doors and on up to the bar counter.

"Gentlemen," Mr. Rodríguez said, "let us go to the work of the coffin before taking tequila."

But Alfredo insisted that one or two quick *tragos* (swigs) would

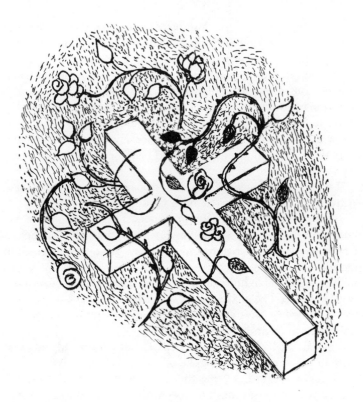

give him the strength he needed for the work. Fortunately we were soon on our way to the workshop again. When we reached its closed door, in the middle of the block on López Cotilla Street, Alfredo felt under a brick in the walk for the key. He turned the brick over only to find that the key was not there.

But luck was with us. At this point, a little boy ran up explaining that he had been using the key as a hammer but had put it back under the brick. He picked up a brick next to the one Alfredo had moved, and showed us the key. Alfredo inserted the large key into the lock and opened the door.

There in the passageway, resting on two sawhorses and glowing in the afternoon light, was Mr. Rodríguez's coffin. It was white, for it had received one thin coat of paint, through which the coarse grain of its pine boards could be seen. We all watched as Alfredo now took up a screwdriver and began to fasten on the last floorboard.

"Now it lacks only the cross with the entwined roses on top," he said. "Then it can be taken to the holy ground. I have promised Mr. Rodríguez that it will have a cross with pink roses."

But in the end it was Lowelito who took the brush and painted the white cross with the pink roses, for after those last two drinks of tequila, Alfredo's hand was too unsteady for that artistic work. Now, to everyone's relief, the coffin was finished. It was turned over to Mr. Rodríguez, and the *cargador* then lifted it up onto his head. Not until he started carrying the coffin did we realize that he, too, had been drinking tequila. We watched him stagger up the street, and it seemed to me that somehow the rhythm of the lines of the pink roses extended down into his legs. Mr. Rodríguez walked in the street alongside the *cargador*, perhaps to make sure that the coffin would not fall onto the cobblestones and be broken.

CHAPTER THREE

San Cristóbal de las Casas

After I had made several drawings of the authentic clay figurines in Isidoro's patio, Lowelito and I were ready to continue our journey into southern Mexico. I wanted to make the drawings to be certain that what I had observed many years before about the spatial order of the figurines had been correct. My theory was that when the ancient artists of western Mexico represented an object, their attention jumped rapidly from point to point within that object.

Isidoro and Alfredo accompanied us to the Guadalajara airport. After promising them that we would return as often as possible, we caught a plane and went by way of Mexico City to the city of Tuxtla Gutiérrez, in Mexico's southernmost state of Chiapas.

I would now be making my first visit to this part of southern Mexico. The feeling I had while in Tehuantepec with Eileen — that southern Mexico was radically different from the rest of the nation — seemed to be the same upon my arrival in Tuxtla Gutiérrez, some miles southeast of Tehuantepec.

In coming to Tuxtla Gutiérrez, Lowelito and I were on our way to the old Mayan ruin of Palenque, farther east in this same state of Chiapas. But realizing that a good place to observe the tribal descendants of the ancient Mayas was in and around San Cristóbal de las Casas, some forty miles from Tuxtla Gutiérrez, we decided to get up to that high city in the mountains as soon as possible.

We went by bus up to San Cristóbal de las Casas. The little Mexican vehicle struggled slowly up the steep, continuous grades and the many hairpin turns. The moment we arrived in that old colonial city, we saw that we had been right in coming, for in addition to the charm of the place, Indians were on all sides, wherever we looked. There was a bewildering number of distinct groups, each with its own kind of costume, moving through the streets.

Each group represented an Indian tribe, and each tribe had its own village. Some villages, such as Chamula and Zinacantán, are but a few miles from the city. Others are situated long distances away. Regardless of the distance, however, Indians from all the villages came regularly to the marketplace in San Cristóbal. Seeing so many distinct Indian groups there gives rise to a natural impulse to try to classify them. People without academic knowledge may resort to their own personal methods, as did a certain Texas tourist we met there. She pointed them all out to me.

"Those over there," she informed me, "are the 'Boys from the Mountains,' and those other two groups to their left are the 'Boys from the Flats' and the 'Boys from the Bushes.' That other bunch over yonder," she continued, "I call the 'Droopy-Drawers Boys.'" This last category embraced the Huixtecas, whose short *pantalones* were noticeably inclined to sag in the rear.

.   .   .

Not long after Lowelito and I arrived in San Cristóbal, we met a pleasant man named Salórzano. A Spaniard, he ran a little store in the middle of a block on a side street near the main plaza. I was attracted to his store by a hand-made Indian harp that I could see through his window. Because of that harp (which I now own) I got to know Señor Salórzano and learned he had an old, beat-up truck with very large wheels. The truck, he said, could take us to Zinacantán, so, early one morning we headed for that village, driving over bad roads, some of them very steep. Salórzano and I rode standing up in the back of the truck. Lowelito rode inside the cab with the driver. Time and again as we went along, the limbs of trees were so low that we had to duck to keep from being knocked out of the truck. There were so many beautiful wild orchids growing on the limbs that I could not refrain from collecting some of them as we bounced along.

At one place, we drove down a steep hill. By the time we got to the bottom of it, we were going very slowly. Just then the road started up again abruptly. Señor Salórzano was standing at the back of the truck bed when the driver suddenly stepped on the gas. To my surprise — and Señor Salórzano's — he shot backward into the air like a big loaf of bread. I thought he would be badly hurt, the truck bed being so high and the hillside so steep, but he must have been an athlete or a bullfighter before he came to Mexico. He flipped both feet high over his head and came down gracefully, feetfirst, on the road. Knowing his abilities made me

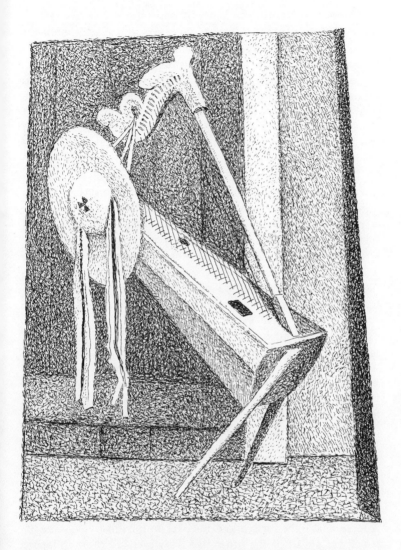

feel more secure as we approached Zinacantán, a village whose inhabitants were notorious for not liking foreigners.

As we came in sight of the village, which was in a beautiful valley, we noticed quite a number of Indians driving little black mules with small wooden kegs strapped to their backs. Señor Salórzano told us that the kegs were filled with an alcoholic drink because a big fiesta was starting that day.

Sometimes I have thought that Alfredo was right when he said Lowelito's ancestor was an Indian named Quetzalcoatl, the nature god for whom the Aztecs mistook Cortés. Lowelito was happiest when he was among Indians. So when we entered the village of Zinacantán in Señor Salórzano's old truck, Lowelito was out of the cab and on the ground before we had come to a full stop.

The fiesta was already going. *Cohuetes* (skyrockets) were being fired into the air at intervals, but nobody was drunk yet, so there did not seem to be any danger. Lowelito had his camera hanging around his neck like a typical tourist, and before I knew it he had disappeared among the Indians.

At that moment the Indians were organizing a horse race at one end of the village. Later we discovered that that was where Lowelito had gone, to get pictures of the race. I saw the event myself and found it not only interesting but also different from any horse race I had ever seen or heard of.

Each contestant had his own horse, and in addition he was given a jug of the alcoholic drink that had come in those kegs carried on the backs of the little black mules. Before the race started, an official handed the riders these jugs and instructed them to drink the liquor before mounting their ponies. When all the riders had drunk the liquor, the signal was given and the race began. But the horses did not start at the same time. Some riders were now so drunk that they had difficulty getting onto their ponies. A few never did make it. Only fifteen or twenty managed to get mounted, and they took off separately down the course at a full gallop. Along the way certain ones would fall off and lie quietly where they fell. Only three riders that day went to the end of the course, made the turn, and came back to the finish line. One arrived far ahead of the other two. However, all three collapsed upon dismounting; none was in a condition to receive any prize — had one been available. The fiesta had begun in a big way, but I was concerned because I could not find Lowelito.

These Indians were different. They were not the kind Lowelito knew so well in western Mexico. The Indians of Zinacantán did

not speak Spanish, nor did they seem to like strangers. It did not matter how much Lowelito liked them. They would not know that Lowelito liked them, nor would they respond to him the way his less primitive Indian friends did.

Now that the *cohuetes* were being fired off in all directions from the bare hands of the drunken Indians, I asked Señor Salórzano to help me find Lowelito.

Near the far end of the village was a raised *ramada* with a ceiling, or roof, made of thatch. The floor of this room was at least six feet higher than the surrounding ground. Here, on this covered platform, the village elders held court, dressed in costumes that contrasted clearly with those of the rest of the population. Each of these stern-looking old Indians always held a staff, the symbol of his authority. Indians charged with crimes were brought before these elders, who passed judgment upon them, finding them guilty or not guilty and, if guilty, setting the punishment they were to receive, which often was a sound and painful flogging.

It was toward this raised platform that Señor Salórzano moved.

Apparently he feared the worst, but I kept looking on all sides for Lowelito as we made our way through the crowd of men and women, many of the latter with babies strapped to their backs or hanging in *rebozos.*

We had not gone far when I saw ahead of us the raised platform and the old men sitting in a row, holding their long sticks, and wearing red headdresses and black coats. When I saw Lowelito seated right in the middle of the old men, I felt sure that all was not right.

Lowelito, the innocent admirer of Indians, had been arrested for snapping all those pictures of the horse race. He had been brought before these judges, and there he was up on a stage sitting among them, waiting to hear his fate. The thought of Lowelito, his shirt removed, being tied to a pole and given lashes with a cowhide whip seemed incredible. But this fiesta was for the Zinacantán people, not for tourists. It was a serious matter. These people were getting drunk, not for nothing, but for religious purposes. I even imagined that with Lowelito captured the way he was, these Indians might decide to revive their old practice of human sacrifice.

I moved up close with Señor Salórzano to observe the procedure. Lowelito had not seen me, but it was clear that, far from being frightened, he was enjoying the whole situation as though he were the honored guest of the judges. He was smiling broadly, and laughing. At times he would slap one of the old men on the knee. As I watched him, dumbfounded, he even took hold of one of the sacred staffs, got it into his own hand, and held it up as though he had just been appointed one of the judges. The old men looked bewildered. Several of them appeared to be lecturing Lowelito, but he smiled back at them and slapped them on their bare knees and laughed.

Just as I was about to give up all hope, the judges suddenly stood up and formed a circle around Lowelito, like one of the huddles football players go into on the field. Lowelito was in the middle of the huddle. We could not see him at all. Now I was certain they had decided to scalp him; I was afraid that he would come out of the huddle lacking his hair and with a bloody head. But when the huddle came apart, I could see that the judges were now laughing as much as Lowelito. They all began to descend the side stairway together. Lowelito had each arm around a judge as all of them went off together and were lost from our view in the crowd. In the late afternoon Lowelito turned up at the truck, and we all returned to San Cristóbal.

. . .

Anthropologists have said that the Indian tribes in this area speak dialects of the ancient Mayan language, as though the many dialects sprang from a single Mayan tongue. Regardless of how the dialects came about, to hear a group of these Indians talking among themselves is certainly a curious experience: the sound is so much like English that one is continuously frustrated by being unable to discover meaning in it.

I began going to the main plaza of San Cristóbal in the very early morning to draw a beautiful blue façade. A veritable sea of Indians would gather and squat around me chattering continuously in their incomprehensible "English." None of the conversation, however, was directed at me. I was not even noticed. I might as well have been a bush growing there. During all the days I was drawing there, not once did an Indian so much as peer over my shoulder to see what I was doing.

In contrast to this attitude was that of the mestizos. By eight o'clock each morning the Indians had moved on. Then the Mexican people, mostly youths going to school, would start passing by. Very soon my presence would cause such congestion that the thought of continuing my drawing was out of the question. My view would be blocked, there would be no elbow room, and all those Mexicans would be talking to me and asking questions in their Spanish language.

The Spaniards and Indians certainly have not always stayed apart, for most of the population of Mexico is now mestizo. Here in San Cristóbal, however, Indians and non-Indians were as distinct as schools of fish in an aquarium.

. . .

San Cristóbal de las Casas does not mean "San Cristóbal of the Houses," as some people might infer. Here the words *las casas* refer to that sixteenth-century champion of Indians, the scholarly bishop of Chiapas, Bartolomé de las Casas. It was to this place that he came in the year 1544 to serve as bishop, but he found such opposition, among both the clergy and the vested interests, that after three years he returned to Spain and carried on his fight from there. His beautiful church is standing yet in the old city. It is fitting that this church should be one of the masterpieces of Spanish colonial architecture, Las Casas being one of the few really humane Spaniards to set foot on Mexican soil in the sixteenth century. The city that bears his name has been called by several other names since its founding in 1522, but the present name seems the proper one: it attracts attention to the city, while the natural beauty of San Cristóbal is a monument fitting to a great man.

This old city is in a high, fertile mountain valley surrounded by still higher hills. Walking in its endlessly charming streets, one is constantly aware of the natural setting. This is not a city that draws itself apart from nature; it does not try to blot out the star-filled sky or the solid earth. Those forces above and below man are a part of the way one experiences San Cristóbal de las Casas. Here, regardless of the high altitude and corresponding flora, one can find reminders of the jungle and tropical lands that lie far below. It is as though this place had been elevated by the jungle onto a high throne, or set like a Mayan temple upon a mountain pyramid. It is a clean little city, with a plentiful supply of water. When Lowelito and I arrived, the place seemed very isolated, but we soon learned that the people living there did not feel that way about it. To them it was the very center of things.

Lowelito and I began exploring San Cristóbal. Walking through its streets we soon learned that each of its *barrios*, or wards, was known for a certain type of work or a certain kind of object manufactured there. In one part of town were the carpenters and cabinetmakers; in another everybody made skyrockets for the fiestas. In still another, the blacksmith's trade was flourishing. Of all the different craftsmen, the blacksmiths, in my opinion, deserved the medal of honor. They were making a great many works of art, no two of which were exactly alike and all of which were in plain public view. Sticking upright on the roof of every house in the city, and even on the Indian grass houses in the suburbs, were

beautiful iron crosses. But they were not ordinary geometric crosses, with just a vertical body and two arms. At times they were as delicate in appearance as lace or a spider's web. They were iron crosses that had been elaborated upon by artists of imagination and taste. These lacy objects afforded endless delight in their variety and grace. If a person thought he might like to take a cross home with him, though, he would find not a single one for sale. After sketching the kind of cross he wanted, he would have to put in an order and wait until the blacksmith got around to making it.

As Lowelito and I walked through the streets of the city, we often entertained ourselves by looking at those crosses, like so many large snowflakes. We began comparing them and their significance with all those things then appearing on rooftops in the United States. Lowelito commented that, like TV antennas, the metal objects on the San Cristóbal houses also carried a message through the roofs and into the interiors. But the message was a different one. Nor did it have a commercial sponsor.

. . .

In 1950 there were only two hotels in San Cristóbal. Lowelito and I chose the one called the Hotel Español, because we preferred its intimacy and small size. After living in the hotel awhile, though, we appreciated it for many other reasons, not the least of which was the delicious food served there.

The façade of the Hotel Español was nothing more than a large door flush with the street. But once through that door, one entered a beautiful little sunny patio filled with bright flowers, fruit trees, and grape vines. In the center of the patio, surrounded by the flowers and vines, was a little fountain in which stood a classical figure made of gray lead. From this little figurine spurted forth a stream of clear water. The proprietor of the hotel, a Spaniard, must have been observant, for he told Lowelito that he was considering substituting Bacardi rum for the water in the fountain.

The guest rooms in the hotel were distributed around three sides of the patio, and the dining room was located on the fourth side. It was a most important place, not only because of the delicious food, but also because of the lively conversation during meals. Lowelito and I were pleased, but also surprised, by the intimacy among the hotel guests. It was soon obvious that we, too, had become members of the guest-family. When we entered the dining room for the first time, it was as though we had been away only temporarily. At first I asked myself, "Who are these Americans way down here in southern Mexico who seem to know me?" I had come with a specific and limited purpose, to make drawings and paintings and to observe and study the different Indian groups, but soon it was clear that Lowelito and I, being members of this family, would have to go along with its plans as well as our own.

There was no way to avoid this, even if we had wanted to. The guests were nearly all Americans, but they certainly were not standard types. Included among them was a New Jersey judge, a Californian who had begun studying for the priesthood only to give it up, and a Texas cattleman with his wife and children. (It was the wife of this cattleman who had pointed out to me all the Indian groups when we first arrived in the city.) There were also several Mexican guests, who could not speak English. Some of these were related to the hotel proprietor's wife; one was a coffee planter who had arrived with twenty or thirty little mules and their Indian drivers.

Of all the guests in the hotel, however, Mr. Ransom was by far the most unusual. He was like no one I had ever known. He was completely unintelligible, even though it was clear he was speaking English. Nevertheless, he, like us, was a bona-fide member of the hotel family.

Whenever Mr. Ransom sat with Mexican guests at dinner, he used Spanish, along with some words he may have picked up from the Indians. These he would combine with English words. Yet, even with this rich and varied vocabulary, nothing he said was intelligible—at least not to me, nor I believe, to anyone else. Along with the words he spoke he added many convincing gestures, and his facial expressions were always tense and lively, varying from laughter to disappointment and even sadness. As a result, although I never understood him, I could not help giving his conversation my undivided attention. In fact, he was very popular with all the guests, joining freely with everyone at the dining tables.

It became the custom every morning for the guests to wander separately on business or sightseeing. They would leave the hotel after breakfast, walking slowly and aimlessly, as though they had no specific destination. Lowelito pointed out, however, that most of them returned as though they were about to miss an airplane flight. Their speed, he said, indicated how far they had drifted away from the dining room.

On those daily walks the guests proved to be collectors as well as sightseers. Their rooms became mostly repositories for their acquisitions. It was as though we were a colony of pack rats. Lowelito acquired a raincoat made of cornstalks; I became the owner of a large, hand-made Indian harp. Every guest would bring in those objects which had caught his fancy for whatever reason. The acquisition that far outstripped all others, though, was that of the New Jersey judge. Upon one of his walks he had found an old house in a state of complete disrepair and had bought it. It was large and impressive, but it was a ruin, and the fact that

57

a poor Mexican family had moved into one of its corner rooms could in no way elevate it. Moreover, it was in such a sad state that it could never have been repaired. When we all went with the judge to admire his acquisition, it was obvious that he felt very proud of it, but I imagined that when he returned to a non-Mexican and more practical environment, he would have some difficulty explaining to his wife, and even to himself, just why he had bought that ruin.

Never were the guests of the Hotel Español objective enough to question their motives for collecting those Indian objects. Everyone was under the influence of some strange Mexican spell. In each room, the pile grew larger and higher. We all continued to visit one another's collections or to carry our newest acquisitions around to the other guests for their admiration.

One little procedure must have been an important part of those exhibitions. It was one I had never witnessed in any art museum. With each viewing, we all drank a wine called *comiteco*, a wine that proved conducive to conversation. It was the same kind of wine that had arrived in Zinacantán on the backs of the little black mules.

On one of those occasions, the subject of "sound" had arisen. Mr. Bill Dugat, the Texas cattleman, was of the opinion that certain sounds, such as the chirping of birds and the ringing of bells, are a kind of natural music, whereas other sounds, such as the barking of dogs, are disagreeable and have no music about them. He said that many poets had remarked upon the music of bells and the singing of birds, but that he knew of no poet who had ever praised the barking of dogs or the hooting of owls. What Mr. Dugat said helped me realize that I associated special sounds with specific places in Mexico. Chapala and Ajijic, for example, were for me places of braying donkeys. I could not recall any poem about the braying of donkeys, but to me that was always a pleasing sound. Although the barking of dogs might not be regarded as musical, it surely can provoke a distinct mood when heard coming from distant places and far into the night. Guanajuato, of course, is a place where the sound of many bells is most pleasant. In Mexico City during some of my walks with Eileen in the lonely Pedregal, I learned that the absence of sound can be a delightful characteristic.

Mr. Ransom brought this conversation on sounds to a close by injecting into it certain word-sounds none of us could understand. Yet, as usual, he did it in a way that held our attention. It seemed to me that what he was trying to say was that people often make the comment, "Seeing is believing" but never say, "Hearing is believing."

.   .   .

When Mrs. Frans Blom, the wife of the famous anthropologist and archaeologist, came to dinner at the hotel one night, she told Mr. Dugat that she disliked Texans and that she hoped he was an exceptional one. Her dislike of Texans was the result of contacts with certain cowboys sent to Mexico by the U.S. government to help combat a cattle disease known as *aftosa*. All those cowboys, she said, held the notion that Texas was still engaged in a war of independence from Mexico and that the Battle of the Alamo was still raging in San Antonio.

Mrs. Blom knew that all Texans were not like that; nevertheless, those she had known were. One evening when she came to dinner, she showed us some of her beautiful photographs of the Lacandón Indians. She knew those jungle Indians well, often visiting them with her husband. On this night, after we all had looked at the photographs, Mr. Dugat, the Texas cattleman, asked to be permitted to keep them for a couple of days. Mrs. Blom laughingly answered that perhaps she would lose them by leaving them with a Texan. Of course we all knew that she was joking. Sitting around the big fireplace, we all continued looking at the pictures.

As the gathering began to disperse, Mr. Ransom asked if he could take the pictures to his own room for the night. Most of us heard him make this request of Mr. Dugat, so as we went to our respective rooms, I was under the impression that the photographs had now passed from Mrs. Blom to Mr. Dugat and on to Mr. Ransom.

The next afternoon, when I had hurried back for the afternoon meal, there was Mr. Dugat in the patio looking very serious. He called to me and told me that when he had asked Mr. Ransom for the photographs, Mr. Ransom had said, "What photographs?" He had said, furthermore, that he had not taken them and that he had not even asked permission to take them. For once, Mr. Ransom had made his meaning clear.

Mr. Dugat was now acting like a Texan—with total directness—in the way he proposed to get the photographs back. By dinner time that night, the situation had been considered by everybody and various suggestions had been made.

It seemed to all of us that this was a matter to be handled with delicacy. The New Jersey judge held that if it turned out Mr. Ransom was a kleptomaniac, then to pin him down and accuse him might do him irreparable psychological harm. Mr. Dugat, however, had only one interest, which was to get those photographs back.

After a short while, Mr. Ransom showed up in the patio. Hoping to keep the situation from getting out of hand, I went over to discuss the problem with him.

"Mr. Ransom," I began, "Mr. Dugat says he can't find the photographs and that he gave them to you last night."

"What photographs? You can search my room," he replied. Then he began to speak less intelligibly and to look through all the magazines on the tables and under everything in the sitting room.

"I am sure you don't remember taking the photographs," I persisted, "but I do distinctly remember that you asked Mr. Dugat for them."

At this, Mr. Ransom appeared bewildered and hurt, and he sped up his search among the old magazines and newspapers. Then he went back to his room.

That evening at dinner, everybody reviewed the case, but poor Mr. Ransom did not even come to dinner. I did get a glimpse of him from the dining room, however. He was going through all the old magazines again.

The judge still held the same opinion that to accuse him, as Mr. Dugat insisted on doing, would be very bad psychologically. The judge also told us that he had been invited by Mr. Ransom to search his room and that he had found no photographs. That, said

Mr. Dugat, didn't mean anything. After a while, we all went back to our rooms.

During this time, Lowelito had not made any suggestions, which was natural since it was always his way to let other people do most of the talking. Now, in our room, he said that he believed he knew who had the photographs.

"I think the New Jersey judge has them," he said.

This was such a novel idea and struck me as being so funny that I could not keep it to myself. I went and knocked on the Dugats' door and told them Lowelito's theory. We had a good laugh out of that one.

When I came back to my room it suddenly occurred to me that someone might get to thinking I had taken them. After all, it was known that I had a special interest in the Indians. The fact remained, though, that we all had heard Mr. Ransom ask for the photographs, and several guests had said they actually saw him go off to his room with them.

Suddenly someone knocked on our door. It was the son of Mr. Dugat.

"What do you think?" he said. "Dad just found the photographs. They were in the bedstand in his own room. He has gone now to Mr. Ransom's room to apologize to him. Mama made him."

A few minutes later, Mr. Dugat arrived looking rather sheepish.

"The damn photographs were in that damn thing by my bed," he began. "But, hell, I looked in it a dozen times, even though for years I never would put anything in those damn things, for fear of forgetting it."

From then on, Mr. Ransom reminded me of the philosopher in Chapala, years before. Having every right to treat us like scoundrels and to make us come crawling, Mr. Ransom now went out of his way to show us how much he liked us. Even so, in his friendliness it is just possible that he knew he was making all of us feel as guilty as dogs.

.   .   .

Living in the Hotel Español with all those American "pack rats" was so fascinating that Lowelito and I seemed to be forgetting that our main destination was the old Mayan city of Palenque, over in the jungle. The time had come to continue our journey.

In those days the bus departed from the other hotel in San Cristóbal. That it departed from there and not from the Hotel Español may indicate the difference between those two hotels. One had to walk from the Español to the other hotel in order to get on the bus. From the Español, however, mules often departed, and when not departing they were just passing through the cobblestone street upon which that hotel opened.

After purchasing our tickets, Lowelito and I had to wait a long time before the bus appeared. As we waited, more and more people arrived and started waiting with us. After a while, I could see that if all those people who were waiting — and we — were going to ride down to Tuxtla Gutiérrez, it was going to be a very crowded bus. In fact, I had never seen a bus in all Mexico large enough to transport so many people. Because we were foreigners, I was not sure but that we would be among those left behind, even though we did own tickets. In addition to all the people, a mountain of luggage had accumulated around the doorway of the hotel. Yet despite the fact that more people with their baggage kept coming, no one appeared perturbed except us.

All along the walls inside the wide-open patio of this other hotel were enlarged photographs of Lacandón Indians. They were enlargements of the same pictures Mr. Dugat had borrowed from Mrs. Blom. These were recent enlargements of her work, and I imagined they had been placed along the walls to help keep Americans from becoming frantic over the multitude of people arriving to ride with them in the little bus down the steep mountainsides to Tuxtla Gutiérrez.

Finally, after the street in front of the hotel had also filled with people, a little blue *camión* suddenly appeared before the doorway. Without much hope, Lowelito and I followed the small boy who, despite his size, had coaxed us into a contract to load our luggage. To our surprise, with hardly any effort we soon were not only inside the bus but also seated. Within a few moments the luggage was loaded into the rear and onto the top. Then, when the little bus pulled away, we saw that riding with us were only five other passengers. Left behind around the hotel doorway, the great crowd was still moving about.

As we started down the mountains, I saw that San Cristóbal de las Casas was just a sort of kite up there, and that the long string which prevented it from flying off to the moon was the thin highway reaching down to Tuxtla Gutiérrez, forty miles below.

.   .   .

In 1950 the city of Tuxtla Gutiérrez, capital of the state of Chiapas, also had only two hotels — or at least only two major ones. Because Lowelito and I would have to remain in that place until we could find someone with an airplane to take us to Palenque, we decided to go to the better hotel — the Bonampak — even though it was on the outskirts of town. Fortunately, the hotel had a couple of station wagons to carry guests back and forth from the city.

I told Lowelito that I hated to be so far out that we could not hear any bells ringing. As it turned out, however, there was another kind of sound to take the place of bells, for just across the street was an old penitentiary full of convicts who seemed to spend their time blowing bugles instead of breaking rocks. Most of the time the bugles sounded inside the building, producing a muffled effect, but in the early morning and the late afternoon the inmates marched outside with their bugles and blew them in front of the penitentiary. They kept this up for about a half-hour or more, and then they lined up and marched back into the building, blowing as they went. The big door then closed behind them, but the muffled sound of bugles could still be heard through the walls. At first we wondered if this practice might have been an unusual form of punishment for the prisoners' crimes. But after watching the men outside we were convinced that this could not be, for it was evident that each and every convict was a bugler from the heart.

CHAPTER FOUR

Palenque

It took several days to find a way to get to Palenque from Tuxtla Gutiérrez. I do not know how, but Lowelito found a man with a small plane who would take us to that old ruined Mayan city. I then went with Lowelito to discuss the trip with this man. He told us that he flew often to the modern village of Palenque. He also assured us that there was a hotel in the village, although *no de lujo* (not luxurious).

We went back to the Hotel Bonampak, happy over our prospective trip. On the way, Lowelito stopped in a fruit market to buy a pineapple. When he came out of the market, he said to me, "Palenque is not going to be at all the way you think." When I did not respond he went on.

"You may get a shock," he said, "because of all your studying. Nobody's imaginary idea of a place is the way it is. That's why I don't make up my mind ahead of time."

Lowelito thought that all the reading I had done about Palenque before going there was a waste of time. I had not only read a lot;

I had also studied photographs and floor plans of the buildings until a clear picture of the place was in my mind. I was sure I would find this picture when I got there. But Lowelito felt certain Palenque would not conform to my preconception. We would soon find out, I said, for we would be leaving the next morning, before seven o'clock.

I did not like the looks of the airplane we boarded. It seemed to have awkward proportions, and there was something artificial-looking about it, but I climbed right into it, ahead of Lowelito.

The most striking thing about the interior of the plane was that it had taken on the appearance of a second-class Mexican train coach, the kind I had seen when Eileen and I went down into the Isthmus of Tehuantepec, in 1927. Old, worn benches were along the two sides, and a variety of objects were stuffed beneath them. There were blankets and packages of all sorts in the aisle between, along with three chickens whose feet were tied together with cord. I was surprised to notice that those hobbled chickens had startled expressions on their faces.

We had barely got off the ground when I saw that we surely must be going to Palenque, for in the pilot's seat up front sat an Indian whose stone-relief portrait appears many times in Mayan art, especially on the walls of the temples at Palenque. I felt that if anyone should know the way to that old Mayan city in the jungle, it should be this Mayan pilot. The only other people with us on the flight were a Mexican coffee planter, his invalid wife, and an Indian maidservant, whom they might have acquired in Tuxtla. By now the maidservant had buried her face in her arms and was trembling all over with fright. The coffee planter scolded her, calling her a *llorona*, or crybaby.

The little plane circled over the city of Tuxtla Gutiérrez several times to gain sufficient altitude, for the nearby mountains were high and the plane bound for Palenque had to get over them. Because we were afraid some of the packages would go flying out into space, the coffee planter and I now tried to close the large side door of the plane. It was not flapping about much, but it was wide open. Standing as though on a high moving platform or a flying carpet, we each tried to close the door, until the pilot motioned to us that the latch was broken and that we might as well leave the door alone. He put his two fists together and abruptly turned them downward in a jerking movement, and then pointed at the door. I knew exactly what he meant, as though he had been speaking English.

Our little plane finally made the summit, but that must have been about its ceiling, for we skimmed so low over the pine trees up there that we could have seen birds sitting in them. Soon we came to a place where the cliffs rose high above us. We were flying through a fairly wide canyon. I noticed that our pilot was peering down, apparently looking for landmarks as we flew along.

All of a sudden we were very high over a deep enclosed valley in the center of which was a little white village. As I was thinking how only a helicopter could descend to it, our plane began to bank and circle. We were really going to try to land there after all. Eventually we came in toward the village from the north. When low, we could see that the village was situated in a narrow gorge with an extremely narrow entrance. As we swept through this aperture, I was pleased that the plane had such short, stubby wings, a feature that had disturbed me when I first saw the plane. The place where we were now landing was the village of Yajalón. To get to it in 1950, one could choose to ride a horse or burro, walk, or ride in an airplane such as ours. But to leave, one had still another choice.

There in Yajalón our traveling companion, the coffee planter, disembarked with his delicate wife and his frightened maidservant. Waiting to carry the coffee planter's wife to their home was an Indian with a comfortable chair strapped to his back. To protect her from the sunlight, an elaborate canopy rose above the chair. Fascinated, we watched as the lady was placed in the chair and then carried off over the hill, the Indian bent slightly forward under his burden. The coffee planter and the maidservant followed behind. We knew that this unique mode of travel was employed when John Lloyd Stephens had passed this way, in the year 1840. We were also reminded of pictures painted on pottery and on the walls of temples, the work of Mayan artists of this area in the early years of the Christian era.

A day or so before our departure from San Cristóbal, Lowelito and I had had the good fortune to spend an afternoon with Don Francisco Blom. During our visit with him, he told us a story about this way of traveling in a chair on an Indian's back. He said that once he came upon an Indian with such a chair strapped to his back in which rode a Spanish lady. This was near Yajalón. The lady was upset because the Indian carrier had met up with a friend who had a bottle of *aguardiente*, and the two of them were walking along together getting drunk. The Spanish lady was helpless because she could not get out of the chair. When Frans Blom came up to them, the Indian carrier was saying to his passenger as he swayed from side to side, "Don't worry, *mamacita*, we are talking business," whereupon up would go the bottle again. Frans rescued the lady, had her get behind him on his horse, and took her to her hacienda.

Our next stop was a place called Salto de Agua, which was under water when we arrived. We landed in a field there, among a herd of cows. The water splashed all around us, but no harm was done. Apparently, landing a plane in a cow pasture under water was no problem to our Mayan pilot, who, we were told later, had once landed his plane in the treetops of a Mexican jungle.

It was when we had left Salto de Agua and were flying perhaps two thousand feet above the jungle that we noticed the chickens were loose. They were free of the cords that had held them together on the floor and were walking around. The chickens must have belonged to the pilot, because Lowelito and I were now the only passengers left on the plane. It seemed to me that I should catch them and tie their feet together again. As I crept toward the big white rooster with a golden ring around his neck, he moved to the very edge of the plane's floor and seemed to be taking a look through the open door at the jungle below. It was inconceivable to me that he would fly out if I pressed him. However, I soon learned that over the years I had been underestimating the spirit of a chicken, for before I could get my hands on him, out the door he went. As long as I could, I watched his soaring, circular descent, and I believe he made the trip down successfully. As I watched him going down, it seemed to me that I was witnessing one of the most remarkable flights ever made by a domesticated fowl. I felt very sympathetic toward that rooster, and I hoped he would not only land safely, but, no other chickens being down there, that he might find some jungle fowl—perhaps a Quetzal bird—to show him how to survive in a jungle environment.

Shortly after the rooster's flight, the pilot caught my attention and pointed toward the west, motioning for me to look in that direction. What I saw was a row of small gray shapes backed up by the deep green jungle. I knew at once that I was seeing some of the buildings of the ancient Mayan city of Palenque. The image itself revealed very little, but its significance filled me with excitement.

"There's Palenque!" I shouted to Lowelito.

A few moments later we slid out of the little canvas-covered airplane into the scrubby cornfield where it had landed. I thanked the pilot and told him not to forget to return for us in two weeks. He smiled and waved as he took off toward the eastern horizon, leaving Lowelito and me stranded in what was for us a strange land. What we were seeing around us was different from anything we had seen before in Mexico.

On the edge of the cornfield, a short distance away, was a small house, and it being the only human sign in sight, we walked over to it. It was made of straw and mud and was entirely open on

one side. Within the house, people seemed to be cooking and washing dishes; outside, a couple of dogs were trying to stay in the
very narrow shade cast by the slightly overhanging straw roof.
Soon the people in the house started eating at little unpainted gray

tables, while Lowelito and I stood outside watching them. Finally, a young Indian woman came out.

Where are you going?" she asked.

"Oh, we are going to Palenque," we answered. "We are just waiting for the bus."

"What bus?"

"Well, then, how far is the village of Palenque from here?" I asked.

"*Pues*, it is about an hour to walk. I will be glad to walk with you. But where will you stay in the village?"

"We will stay in the hotel, of course," I assured her.

"What hotel?" said she.

By asking us a very few questions, this girl had taught us a lot about the village of Palenque. We found that in Palenque there was no hotel nor anything approaching one, *de lujo* or *no de lujo*. Nor was there a restaurant, and food was scarce in the homes of the people.

. . .

Lowelito and I had fully expected to find some kind of lodging in the village of Palenque. The man who owned the airplane had led us to believe that there was a hotel available. Certainly we were not equipped for camping. We looked up and down the village street lined with flimsy houses and noticed that at the end of the street was one building that had been solidly constructed with stone. When we were closer, we discovered it was an old abandoned church. To out delight it turned out to be entirely vacant except for a goat. This building would have to serve as a private hotel. The fact that it lacked a roof was a disappointment, especially because the rainy season was beginning. The building also lacked a floor. High weeds were growing all over its interior. Under the circumstances, though, it looked promising. And it did have one charming feature: On either side of its spacious entranceway, set into the wall, was a large carved stone panel. These panels were masterpieces of classic Mayan relief sculpture. We knew they had been brought from the old Mayan city of Palenque, some twelve miles beyond the edge of the jungle.

Our hotel in this abandoned church was lacking in every comfort except one on our first night as guests there. Because we slept in the weeds in one corner of this large structure, the rainfall during the night did not reach us. But because that rain had been only a drizzle, I decided next morning to make improvements on our adopted home. Noticing that the houses up and down the street were built of straw and sticks, I imagined that we could construct a small lean-to of such materials in one corner of the old building. I sent Lowelito out to look for some poles and sticks. But just as I was leaving in search of straw, an Indian boy arrived with a message that brought our architectural plans to an abrupt conclusion. In some mysterious way the news had spread that two North Americans had arrived and begun living in the church. The message brought to us by the Indian was that "Don Ernesto" would expect us to stay at his hacienda, and that we should arrive in time for supper.

This good news gave us such a feeling of security that we left our dry corner in the old church, said good-bye to our hotel companion, the church goat, and went out to learn about the village. Lowelito was especially interested in finding a cantina, for he said he never felt completely secure if he did not have a bottle handy with which to offer a drink to anyone who might be doing us a favor. The Indian messenger had told us how to get to Don Ernesto's hacienda, which was about a mile from the village, and we took care to leave in time to arrive there and not be late for supper.

Don Ernesto proved to be an elderly German gentleman. He had lived there through all the Mexican revolutions. The bullet holes he showed us in his house were proof enough of what had gone on during his residency. We also learned that before coming to Mexico he had fought in the Spanish-American War. He told us that after escaping from Germany to avoid compulsory military training, he arrived in the United States just as the Spanish-American War was beginning. By some trick of fate, he soon found himself in the U.S. Army fighting Spaniards. Thereafter he went to Mexico and settled on land that soon became a favorite battleground of the conflicting forces of that war-torn country. Because of the battles fought around his house, he had formed the habit of closing all windows and doors each night, despite the tropical heat. This habit he continued to indulge while Lowelito and I resided there with him, and because of it Lowelito said to me several times that he would prefer to be sleeping again with that goat in the church.

In the evenings we would sit on the open porch, where it was cooler. Don Ernesto would talk incessantly. I suspect he would have talked all night if we could have brought ourselves to stay awake and listen. When finally we did indicate our desire to go inside, he would immediately start telling another story, hoping to entice us to remain a while longer on the open porch. He made it difficult for us to retire, but when we did he would follow us reluctantly and then begin nailing up all the solid blinds over the windows and locking the doors. As soon as that had been done, the temperature rose, and we would remember why he was so opposed to going to bed: Almost anything was better than spending the night in an oven.

Once inside the oven, we often wished we had stuck it out on the porch, despite the mosquitoes there. When I suggested one night that I might sleep on the porch, Don Ernesto said he would not permit it. He insisted that if I tried it I would wake up the next morning with my head severed from my body. This, I knew, was absurd; his fear was a carryover from long ago, during the fighting around his house.

The three of us slept in the same small room, a dark, hot dungeon. Two beds were in the room, and each had a mattress stuffed with cornhusks. Besides the heat, then, there was another discomfort: Any movement in the beds made enough noise to awaken even a sound sleeper. As I lay in that dark room, I often thought of the little straw house I had planned to build in the corner of that old roofless Spanish church.

One late afternoon, as we sat on the porch with Don Ernesto, a man rode up on a horse. Don Ernesto greeted him cordially, for he had been waiting impatiently for him to arrive. This man, a civil engineer and also a Frenchman, had come from a town in the neighboring state of Tabasco to survey Don Ernesto's ranch. He was supposed to reside in the ranch house during all the weeks it would take for him to survey the ranch. That night Don Ernesto erected a third bed in our oven, to take care of the French engineer.

This third bed also had a mattress stuffed with cornhusks, and during the sleepless night that followed, with everyone turning over and over, the noise was strange and incessant. The next morning, the Frenchman went with Lowelito and me to the village, where he found a place to sleep each night thereafter in a house that had eight or ten hammocks hanging side by side in the front room. But Lowelito and I decided to stick it out with Don Ernesto.

Usually about the time I would get to sleep, Don Ernesto would get up noisily and go out while it was still dark. Later he told me that for many years his first act upon arising was to go immediately to the creek behind his house and jump into it. I was sure that anyone else living there would eventually acquire the same habit. Nothing could be more logical upon arising from a noisy bed of coals than to rinse off the night's perspiration.

One morning before daylight, after the Frenchman had deserted us, I was startled to observe someone in the room trying to open Don Ernesto's heavy iron safe at the foot of his bed. I could not imagine how anyone had entered the house after Don Ernesto had nailed the windows shut and locked the doors so carefully. With the aid of a dim flashlight, this person was trying to work the combination lock on the safe. I lay there very still. If I moved at all, the cornhusks would make lots of noise, and the man might even attack me to keep me quiet. Soon, however, I discovered that the person was Don Ernesto himself. It must have taken him fully five minutes to open his safe. Finally he pulled the heavy, squeaking door back and, feeling around in the safe, pulled out something I would never have expected: three little white chicken eggs.

. . .

When we had walked to Don Ernesto's hacienda from the village that first day, we had followed a trail cut through a small section of the jungle. This trail led into a clearing at the far end of which was a small creek. It was the same creek that flowed behind Don Ernesto's house, the one in which he washed himself each morning. When we arrived at the creek that day, we removed our shoes, waded across it, and climbed the hill through coconut palms to the ranch house.

Soon, however, we were unable to wade the creek in the mornings. During many nights it rained, and then the creek became a raging torrent. Don Ernesto, however, had foreseen this difficulty. When we arrived at the creek we would find an Indian waiting there with a horse. The horse proved to be an excellent ferryboat. It would ferry me across, swimming part of the way; then, without being urged, it would go back for Lowelito.

From the bank of the creek, we walked to the village. Great flocks of green parrots were in the treetops, quarreling among themselves the way I had known crows to do. They were very talkative and, as Lowelito said, obviously illiterate. From the village of Palenque, we were carried within a short distance of the ruined Mayan city, the first day by *camioneta* (a light truck) and thereafter by jeep. The *camioneta* was said to belong to Don Ernesto's son, who was away at school. The road might have taken us right into the ruins had a bridge not been washed away by the last rains. But this was fortunate for us in that we were forced to walk slowly through the jungle and in that way became better acquainted with it.

The jeep and the *camioneta*, the only two automobiles in the village, had not been there long enough to wear down the grass growing in the street. Palenque village, unlike some Indian villages in the state of Chiapas, did have streets — or at least one street. (There may have been another, but if so I did not see it.) This main street, although straight, was laid out for pedestrians and for people riding mules or burros. The wheel, unused by the ancient Mayan Indians, was even now rarely used in this area.

A description of the village of Palenque written by John Lloyd Stephens in the year 1840 still described the village as Lowelito and I saw it more than a hundred years later. Stephens wrote that a boy could roll on the grass out of the church at the end of the street and continue rolling on grass right up the street and on out of the village. From the description Stephens wrote, it was possible for us to retrace his steps about the village. This does not mean that the houses we saw were the same ones present there a hundred years before. Stephens tells that while in his dwelling one day he heard a loud noise outside, and upon rushing out he saw that a house down the street had suddenly crashed to the ground. Apparently when a building fell down in the village of

Palenque, the people would build another one just like it in the same place. Lowelito said that the architectural style there should be called "ever changing permanence." It occurred to me that a tendency toward that style could be found in all parts of Mexico. When we left Don Ernesto's house the first morning, we had had a good breakfast. He had served us each a fried egg—no doubt one of those he kept in his iron safe—and a bowl of oatmeal with goat's milk. Consequently when we arrived at the village and arranged to be carried by the *camioneta* to the ruins, it never occurred to us to think about lunch. Lowelito had looked everywhere for a cantina, but he had not bothered to look for any food. He continued to complain about having no rum or tequila to offer when anyone might do us a favor.

It was a hot, steaming morning, and although the jungle we had to walk through was dark and cool, the spaces between the pyramids and temples were hot and filled with high weeds. It was sticky hot as we made our way through the weeds and climbed the tall pyramids. Lowelito took many photographs, while I spent my time making drawings and taking notes. We were the only human beings among all the old stone buildings. In those days there were no tourists in the ruined city of Palenque.

By noontime we were very hungry, but of course there was nothing to eat. Lowelito kept busy taking photographs, although I did hear him comment that if only Isidoro were with us he would find some wild cucumbers and make us a lunch. Then I noticed, scattered here and there between the pyramids and temples, some dark green shapes different from the green foliage around them. They seemed to have a "tame" look, and when I went close to them, they turned out to be orange trees loaded with fruit. I filled my hat with the oranges and found Lowelito inside the building called "the Palace Group." Although the fruit was quite sour, it helped us forget our hunger. Later I learned that the orange trees had been planted by Frans Blom several years before, when he was studying the ruins.

When our *camioneta* arrived for us in the late afternoon and honked its horn, the night birds had already started their strange calling. As hungry as we were, we hated to leave.

By now Lowelito had acquired a different motivation. When

we arrived back in the village, he began to ask, not about a cantina, but about a place where we might eat. Walking up the street we met an old man who looked as though he could have been in Palenque during the time of Stephens and his artist companion Frederick Catherwood.

"Señor," Lowelito said, "please pardon me for bothering you and for not having any tequila or rum to offer you, but there does not appear to be a cantina in this beautiful pueblo, and we wonder if you know of a home where the people might let us eat meals with them."

The old man removed his hat out of politeness. He thought for a moment and then, pointing to a place up the street, said, "*Señores*, the lady who lives in that house with the cactus fence, which you can see from here, has a very large and healthy family. She has ten or twelve sons. Some of those sons are married and have children. All of them eat at that lady's house. She has so many eating there that I believe she would be glad to offer you meals."

We thanked him and went immediately to that house. After listening politely to Lowelito, the old mother said we would be welcome to come there each midday for dinner. It was arranged that we would dine with her and her family now and then but that most of the time she would put up a lunch for us to take to the ruins. Feeling much better organized we proceeded to Don Ernesto's ranch house, where we knew we would enjoy our supper.

Walking through the village past our old church-hotel, the only building of stone, we noticed that the houses became even more fragile and impermanent on the edge of the village. We could not help thinking how different the ancient Mayan people were in their ability or ambition to build. While it is true that the common people of ancient times lived in flimsy huts, they did build temples and palaces of stone. The people who live in the area today, although descendants of the ancient ones, do not make such an effort. Lowelito remarked that if the ancient people lived in Palenque today our airplane would have landed on a stone surface instead of in a cornfield.

Of all the qualities noticeable in both the sculpture and the architecture of Palenque, the degree of refinement is perhaps the most impressive. Refinement in proportion is not unusual in primitive art, but at Palenque this quality is remarkable because of its gentle character. The gentle treatment found in the sculpture there, the graceful line at once precise and varied, surely must reveal the character of the people who lived there so long ago. When viewed in terms of personality, this sculpture is gentle, refined, sympathetic, and kind, as well as forceful.

It was obvious that the low-relief sculpture at Palenque, both in plaster on the exterior walls and in stone carving, was richly symbolic. But when the ancient Maya ceased to exist, that symbolism ceased to have meaning. The human figures in the sculpture are recognizable enough, but any further significance was as hidden as was the meaning of most of the hieroglyphic writing. Archaeologists and anthropologists were trying to recover this lost meaning, but for Lowelito and me the inaccessibility of symbolic meaning made it easier for us to give our undivided attention to purely visual qualities. What we found when we attempted to copy the sculpture was almost incredible: Its subtlety and perfection were beyond reproduction.

Despite the high weeds growing between the pyramids and temples, we were able to visualize the arrangement of the buildings well enough to know that the same subtle qualities prevailed there also. Nor would a flat floor plan of this arrangement do it justice: The architects also utilized different levels to achieve their overall architectural effects.

The days spent in the ruins of Palenque, when the place belonged only to us and itself, were filled with fascination. Even so, the absence of Eileen, from whom I could not even receive letters, was beginning to trouble me. Lowelito could have remained there indefinitely; at that time he had no feminine attachments. Unlike me, he did not live with a nagging feeling that the pilot just might forget his promise to come back for us in two weeks.

The rains began to fall more frequently and heavily each day. Often the sky looked as though it were holding as much water as the Pacific Ocean, and only awaiting the order from Chac, the Mayan rain god, to let it out in one grand flood. Consequently, on the appointed day I began scanning the sky in the early morning and continued scanning it even as we walked to the cornfield where the plane would land. When I saw a small black spot just above the horizon in the east, I was both pleased and disturbed. The plane was coming, but it should have been coming from the west. The spot grew larger each second and eventually drew close enough for me to recognize it as our plane. When it touched down among the cornstalks, I thought I had never seen so grand a machine. I knew that its canvas covering had been painted with silver paint, but to me it was now pure silver. Even the swinging door was closed.

The French engineer was flying with us. He and Lowelito had become great friends after discovering a small cantina with a good supply of rum. With that rum to offer people who might be doing him a favor, Lowelito now felt very secure. So secure, in fact, that he thought we should accept the Frenchman's invitation to stop off for a visit at his place in the nearby state of Tabasco. We did agree to have the pilot let the Frenchman off at his village, but after sincere *abrazos* we then said good-bye. Soon the little plane was in the air, and I was on my way back to Eileen, where I belonged.

Further Trips to Baja

What I had seen in Palenque could not be translated into words. Eileen would have to see it with her own eyes — and I was determined to take her there at the first opportunity.

In the meantime, though, there was still Baja California. Eileen was always eager to go there, and just before Thanksgiving in 1950 she said to me, "Let's not bother with a turkey this year. Let's get a couple of steaks and barbecue them on top of Table Mountain."

Her suggestion made me laugh, even though it was so typical of her. I did not know how to get to that mountain, let alone get on top of it. We had seen it many times from the highway south of Tijuana, but I doubted if there were any road leading to it. Nevertheless, I thought she had a good idea, and early on Thanksgiving morning we put the steaks in our station wagon and, along with our Irish setter, set off to see if we could get to Table Mountain and climb to its flat top.

We drove down the Ensenada highway until it appeared to us that we were about even with the mountain. At that point very near the seacoast was the village of Rosarito. There, in a liquor store and a bakery shop, we bought a bottle of Chianti wine and a loaf of Mexican bread to complete our Table Mountain Thanksgiving dinner.

From Rosarito a dirt road led off the highway in an easterly direction. We felt certain it would take us to our destination. We had not gone far when this road forked, one route leading north, the other south. Taking the south fork we soon came to a barbedwire gate. We could see that we were getting closer to the mountain. We were driving through beautiful country, mostly wild but with small corn patches here and there. The only discordant effects were a couple of places where people had dumped piles of tin cans. Eileen commented that those cans looked very offensive. I told her that maybe that was because they didn't belong there, but I knew this could not be the true reason. Eileen never needs any explanation when something pleases or displeases her. The fact that it does is enough in itself. She may say, for instance, that a necktie I have put on is not the right one for my coat and then point out that it has no color in it that is also in the coat, that it has no "relation" to the coat. Giving a reason, however, is done only to prove to me that I should take it off and put another one on. She never gets any pleasure in finding out *why* a thing pleases her or not. Those tin cans piled out there, where nature was otherwise undisturbed, were simply offensive to her, and as far as she was concerned no explanation was called for. Even so I could not help discussing the subject further.

"Those tin cans are certainly in the wrong place," I said, "but if those piles could be surrounded by others for acres and acres around, then they would be in harmony with their surroundings. It would be the same as having a necktie that had something in common with the coat."

This explanation seemed logical to me, and I might have gone on believing it had Eileen not then added her own thought.

"The more tin cans there might be out there, even if they were spread from here to Ensenada, the worse they would look to me," she said.

We were getting closer and closer to our mountain, but because of the trees and canyons it would sometimes be out of sight. Soon we came to a picturesque house under large sycamore trees. Many bright flowers were growing in tin buckets attached to the walls of the house. Eileen said I should make a painting of that scene on some future trip. After driving another mile or so, we came to an adobe house that was near a bright-green live-oak tree, the only live oak in that area. A few yards farther on we made a right-angle turn and came to another barbed-wire gate. Such gates are quite difficult to open and close, so whenever we came to one I would always get out and open it, and let Eileen drive the car through. Then I would close the gate. To leave a gate open would be unthinkable.

For the next mile or two we drove under thick tree foliage and along the edge of a little creek; then suddenly the road forked again. One fork went to the right, under big sycamore trees and over large white boulders. The other went to the left, up a steep hill. We followed the latter road, which kept climbing steeply for about two miles. Then we came out onto a flat meadow at the far end of which was an old adobe house with a barn behind it. The barn had stone walls and a red tile roof. I thought we had better stop at the house and inquire, for the road seemed to end at that place.

After we had called out, a man came around the house. He was a pleasant man. He said he was a Spaniard, and that his name was Fernández. I asked him if it were possible and permissible to go to the top of the mountain. Taking a stick in his hand, he knelt down and began drawing a map for us in the dirt. He showed us how we could go around his barn and find a faint trail that would lead us as far as it was possible to go in an automobile.

That Thanksgiving Day we managed to drive our station wagon up onto the north shoulder of the mountain, where, in a beautiful grove of oak trees, we found a spring of clear cold water that flowed among granite boulders the size of small houses. Many holes had been ground into the boulders, forming *metates* (stone mortars), which showed that this place had been a favored spot of the ancient Indians and that the Indian women had sat on those boulders and ground the acorns and wild seeds into a flour for food.

At this old Indian campsite we were about five hundred feet below the supposedly flat top of the mountain. To get up there was a difficult climb through thick brush and around rock cliffs, but we finally arrived on top. While we were struggling upward our bird dog must have reached the top and returned to us several times. After exploring the top, we saw that it would be impossible for an airplane to land up there. I remembered talking to a man once who told me he often landed his plane there, and now I knew he was a happy liar. But I forgave him, since he told me that lie at a cocktail party. Eileen and I now started back down to the spring.

Eileen is addicted to exploring. I had learned that in Chapala years before, and I have always loved that about her. Regardless of our destination, whenever she sees a road leading off somewhere she will ask me to turn off and see where that road goes. So as I came down from the top of Table Mountain ahead of Eileen, in order to find a better route and make the descent easier for her, I had not gone far through the high thick brush when I discovered that she was not following me. She had found another route, one that was more to her liking. I continued on down, but just as I reached the spring I heard her calling me to come back and help her.

Immediately I began my second ascent, but I found that it would be necessary to go all the way to the top and then start down again in order to get to where Eileen seemed to have stopped. She kept calling to guide me in the right direction. After making my way through the brush and getting scratched by the thorny bushes, I finally came upon her in a thicket, sitting on a boulder that was perched on the edge of a precipice. I asked her what she was doing in that particular spot.

"I was sitting here thinking of how awful those tin cans looked," she said.

There was no way to go forward from that place, so we had to return to the top again. From then on Eileen could truthfully tell her friends that she had been on top of Table Mountain two times, and I could say I had been up there three times.

On the way down this time I insisted that Eileen go in front of me so that I could discourage her from any impulse she might have to explore some trail leading off in another direction.

At the spring we cooked our steaks over a fire made of dry oak

The Road, Baja California

Tepehuanes in Tijuana

The Mission Church, San Ignacio, Baja California

Eileen at Bahía de los Angeles, Baja California

bark. With our wine and Mexican bread we celebrated Thanksgiving. We did not miss Thanksgiving turkey at all. We were both
thankful and happy to be together in such a beautiful and remote
spot, surrounded by clear evidence that Indian people had enjoyed this same place years before the arrival of the white man.
It almost seemed to us there in the silent sunshine that those Indians were celebrating Thanksgiving with us. We knew, however,
that the Indians who had camped in this place so long ago would
never have contributed such produce to our Thanksgiving dinner
as the Indians back East had contributed to the Pilgrims. The Indians in this area lived much like the wild coyotes but were not
as good at hunting. Their food was wild seeds, acorns, perhaps
some rodents and grubworms, and often shellfish from the nearby
ocean. Whatever culture they had was archaic. Nevertheless, as
we sat that day in the shade of great oak trees, among those
boulders by the clear spring, we felt the presence of those Indians
all around us.

.   .   .

One year later, Eileen and I were again traveling alone in Baja,
when suddenly we came upon a dark grove of oak trees. A dirt
road ran through this mysterious grove and on to the sea. Neither
the oak grove nor the dirt road through it is the same now as it
was on that day. Too many people who like to carve their names
on tree trunks have since found the grove. They have camped under the big trees, scattering their beer cans and paper plates, and
they have also lit fires that swept through the grove. Floods have
come, carrying some of the big trees clear to the ocean. Even so,
part of the oak grove is still there.

As we turned off the main road near the foot of the Santo Tomás
grade that first time and went west, we did not think it possible
to find a place more beautiful than what we were seeing. When
we arrived at the entrance to that dark oak grove, we had such
a strong feeling of expectancy that instead of entering it we turned
off the road, intending to camp up a little draw to the right. A
short while later, after a light lunch out of Eileen's basket, we began walking cautiously along the road that led into the dark shadows under the great oak trees. We knew that we were entering

an enchanted place, for we could feel the presence of those nature spirits and genii so well known both to the ancient Greeks and to the primitive Indians of western Mexico.

The shadows were a million rich and varied black shapes scattered over the ground, embraced by an equal number of blindingly brilliant spots of light. As we watched, those dark forms and bright spots seemed to bounce up into the great trees above and then dance about among the tree limbs and leaves. Movement was all around us, above and below, as the lights and shadows were whirling and dancing, swinging and jumping, in a symphony of silence. Surely, I was thinking, this place must be the headquarters of that natural paradise on earth which exists within Baja California. From this enchanted spot the spirits of nature must spread out to all the other unspoiled places in Baja.

We walked about a mile through that cathedral of giant trees until the road led us suddenly out into a sea of bright sunlight. Then we retraced our steps and saw it all over again.

When we arrived back at our station wagon, Eileen said, "Let's see where the road goes."

Leaving our camping equipment up the little draw, we started driving through the grove of dark trees and on west. There were no "tangible" people in the grove, only those unseen ones. Nor were there beer cans or paper plates, and no one had carved his name on the great tree trunks.

Soon after leaving the oak grove, we came to a small house near the dirt road, under sycamore trees. Although it was picturesque, it did not look altogether Mexican to us, so we stopped to inquire.

Before I could knock or call out, the door opened and a friendly man stepped out to greet us. He acted as though he had been expecting us. To our surprise, he looked more like an American businessman or banker than a Mexican farmer.

"Welcome to Santo Tomás Valley," he said. "My name is Marjoram. Very few Americans ever come by my house."

Mr. Marjoram was an American who had come across the border and settled in that spot many years before. He had married a Mexican woman, and at the time of our visit they had five sons. On that day we did not meet his wife or his children, but eventually—on later trips to Baja—we did meet the sons. They looked completely Mexican, despite Mr. Marjoram's very white skin. One of the sons, Francisco (Pancho), looked as though his father could have been Pancho Villa. He grew to be very tall and strong, and to this day he is our good friend. On several occasions we have tried to persuade Pancho to drink less tequila. I once gave him a lecture on the evils of alcohol. I assured him that if he would leave it alone he could become a leader in that part of Baja. Pancho, with a glass in his hand and tears in his eyes, said that only his late father had ever talked to him like that. Then he raised his glass and said, "*Amigo mío*, you are right. Let's drink to my quitting of drinking tequila!"

Eileen and I did not get to know Mr. Marjoram well; he died not long after we first met him. He had asked us to bring along any old magazines or newspapers the next time we were down, which we did. He had said, "Bring any you have. It doesn't matter how old they are. We don't pay much attention to time down here."

On that first day, Eileen and I left Mr. Marjoram's house and drove on to the coast, a distance of about fifteen miles. The view of the sea was exciting there, with high cliffs above the water, and on the cliffs a group of old lobster-fishermen shacks. We then drove back through the mysterious oak grove to where we had piled our equipment, and spent the night there. We knew we had found a place to which we would return. But we did not know that we would return to that place each Thanksgiving Day thereafter for well over thirty years.

. . .

Some months after our discovery of the oak grove, Eileen and I were driving south toward Ensenada with Lowelito. When we came to a place called La Misión, we noticed a dirt road leading off the highway. It went abruptly down into the valley and continued past the ruined adobe walls of an old Spanish mission. When Eileen saw the road, she said, "We have never been over that road and up that valley. Why don't we go see what it's like up there?"

To her delight I immediately turned off the highway onto the dirt road. We followed it for five or six miles, until we came to the biggest sycamore tree I had ever seen, and there we camped.

Sycamore trees are common in the canyons of Baja California, but this one up La Misión Valley was exceptional. It was so large that we were shocked when we looked at it. To me it was more than just a large tree. I saw it as a magnificent "system," complex and subtle. Growing about eight feet above the ground was a branch that extended sixty or seventy feet parallel to the earth's surface. To support this limb the tree had developed a central trunk as big around as a house and anchored with great roots, some going downward and others spreading out over the ground like boa-constrictors.

Late that afternoon, Lowelito hung his hammock under that long, massive limb, which must have weighed several tons. I did not envy him that bed. Made of sisal strings, the hammock looked uncomfortable to me, but Lowelito had become accustomed to sleeping in hammocks while in the Yucatán; in fact he had become very attached to it. As I watched him adjust the ropes, it occurred to me that perhaps he had chosen a dangerous place to sleep. However, when I considered the strength of the trunk I dismissed the thought from my mind.

The next day, a big Mexican cowboy came into our camp. After drinking a cupful of rum that Lowelito had given him, he noticed the hammock swinging under the limb. Apparently he could not resist climbing into the hammock. As soon as he had stretched out comfortably, however, the hammock strings gave way and he was deposited on the ground. Seeing this catastrophe, Lowelito poured himself a cupful of rum. Then he filled another cup and gave it to the cowboy.

"Lowelito," I said, "you certainly are generous to reward that vaquero with a drink for ruining your hammock."

"He had nothing to do with it," Lowelito answered. "The hammock did it for me. It knew I shouldn't be sleeping under that heavy limb, so it broke. It gave up its own life for me."

Lowelito was quiet the rest of that day. He picked up his paint box and stool and walked out of camp, but when he returned he had not painted or even started a picture. In the very late afternoon, I saw him gather up the old hammock and a sack of empty beer bottles. Then he took the hammock and the beer bottles up the riverbed and dug a grave. After putting first the hammock and then the bottles into the grave, he filled the hole with dirt and placed white rocks on top.

"I put those beer bottles in with it," he said, "as an offering to the Mayan god of hammocks."

The moonlight was so bright and the weather so balmy while we camped at the big sycamore tree that we stayed up very late each night talking about the times we had spent together in Mexico. Lowelito also told us of his experiences in Yucatán when he and Jean Charlot were working with the Carnegie Institution's archaeological expedition at Chichén Itzá. As a result of our conversation we decided to return to Chapala as soon as possible, see our old friends Alfredo and Isidoro, and then take Eileen to see Guanajuato. I wanted to include Palenque on the same trip, but because of our jobs we realized that Palenque would have to wait until later.

Having made the decision to return to mainland Mexico, we packed our equipment into the station wagon and started for the border. As we drove northward we knew we were already on our way back to Chapala and that soon Eileen would be seeing Guanajuato for the first time.

CHAPTER SIX

Eileen in Guanajuato

Many times over the years, I have heard people say, "You can't return." What they meant was that you cannot go back to a place you loved and expect to find it as lovely as it was the first time. I do not know how that saying ever got started; in my experience, and Eileen's, it has always proven false. Over the years, we both had returned many times to our favorite places in Baja, and every time we returned we enjoyed those places as much as or even more than before. I had found the same to be true on my 1950 visit to Chapala. Now, two years later, Eileen and I were going back to Chapala, where she would have the opportunity to test that statement at a place where we had spent part of our honeymoon.

Unlike Eileen's first trip down into mainland Mexico, which was by train, this trip was by airplane, and we arrived in Guadalajara in what seemed an unbelievably short time. Immediately we went to Chapala by bus, where we registered at the Hotel Nido. Lowelito was unable to fly down with us, but he had assured us he would join us in two or three days.

When Eileen and I arrived, Isidoro and Alfredo immediately became our constant companions. As usual, Alfredo closed his carpenter shop and refused to take any more orders, even for coffins. Lowelito arrived on schedule. The few days we spent again with our old friends were as magical as those we had enjoyed twenty-six years before. Now Eileen could see that Isidoro was no longer a slim boy and that Alfredo was indeed stockier and bowlegged, as I had told her. It was equally clear to her, however, as it had been to Lowelito and me two years before, that they were really the same as they had been so long ago. The saying "You can't return" was now, for us all, nothing short of nonsense.

As wonderful as this visit to Chapala proved to be, our limited time made it necessary to continue on to Guanajuato. Lowelito and I felt we could show Eileen just about everything there was to see in that old city, having overlooked nothing when we were living there so many years before.

We decided to go from Guadalajara to Guanajuato by bus this time, for we did not want to take the chance of making bad connections on the train. When we entered the bus in Guadalajara in the late afternoon, Eileen led the way to the very back, where we sat on the seat that extended clear across the rear end of the vehicle. I think she chose that position because it would afford her a view of everything that might happen all the way to the front entrance. Eileen does not like to miss anything. Shortly after nightfall, though, I began to doubt the wisdom of her choice of seats, for the bus caught on fire up front. The smoke became so thick up there that we could not even see the driver. I began examining the windows near us to find out if we could escape through them. All the passengers up at the front, however, seemed to be highly entertained. They were all laughing while the driver was struggling to put out the fire with his *cobija* (blanket). In fifteen or twenty minutes the fire was out and we were safe, but I have never chosen to ride in the rear of a bus since then.

I was delighted to think that we would be arriving in Guanajuato in the dead of night, just as Lowelito and I had done in 1925, but I knew that Eileen would not hear the horses' hooves on the cobblestone streets, because the bus probably would deliver us to the center of the city.

Because neither Lowelito nor I could remember the name or the location of the hotel we had stayed in during our first night in Guanajuato, we went to one of the better hotels, on the Plaza de la Unión, only to find it completely full. We were advised to go to the Hotel Orozco, way out by the *presa* (dam). We had never heard of that hotel, but we had a taxi take us there. It was so far out that we could not hear any bells ring during the night. Lowelito commented that there was not even a penitentiary nearby with buglers. The hotel was very comfortable, although completely modern and lacking the old colonial flavor of Guanajuato. Like the Hotel Bonampak in Tuxtla Gutiérrez, the Hotel Orozco had a station wagon available for the guests.

The first day after our arrival, Lowelito and I took Eileen to see what we thought were the most interesting places in the city. The next morning I went down to the hotel lobby and found Eileen already there. She had left our room while I was shaving and had gone down ahead of me. When Lowelito joined us, he remarked that Eileen looked very exhilarated.

"I have some wonderful news for you," she said. "I have just talked to a man, and he has made all arrangements for us to visit one of the old Spanish mines. A driver will pick us up in a car in one hour, so let's hurry and have breakfast!"

When Lowelito and I had lived in Guanajuato before, we had peered cautiously down into the depths of one of those old silver mines, but we certainly had never had the slightest desire to explore any of them. In that old city, we were totally committed to the bright sunlight.

Now Eileen was telling us that she had made arrangements for us to descend into one of the deepest holes of all. She said the man had told her that this mine was still being worked, at least on one of its many levels.

It turned out that she had arranged everything, even though she had preceded me down into the lobby only by as long as it takes me to shave with a safety razor.

The driver arrived, and within an hour we were at the office of the mine, where the management placed us in the care of a young Mexican engineer. This young man handed each of us a helmet and an old-fashioned carbide lantern. He then led us by a trail up over a mountain. I had accepted my lantern with reluctance, and when no one was looking I discarded it altogether. Soon we arrived at the dark entrance of a tunnel, which went horizontally into the mountain. We followed the engineer into this dark hole until it turned a corner. At this point, we all stopped while the carbide lanterns were lighted. I was so embarrassed not to have mine that I ran back and retrieved it. The engineer then lighted mine. The lanterns were burning with a small open flame and seemed to double the size of our little group, for we now had a lot of tall, dark shadows going along with us in the tunnel.

After we had gone a few hundred feet along this horizontal tunnel, we came suddenly to where it opened into a vertical shaft. The way those two holes were hooked together was extremely crude and direct. The vertical one was round and about twenty feet in diameter, and, as near as I could judge without getting too close, it went all the way down to hell. Above, it also seemed to extend to the heavens.

We stood there waiting, and I did not know for what. I noticed an old iron cable about as big as one's index finger in the vertical hole. The engineer took a pair of pliers, reached out, and tapped on the cable.

A few moments later, my attention was drawn to an oversized bucket with three upright bars for sides; it was as if the solid sides of the bucket had been cut away. This quaint object had been tied over against the far side of the vertical tunnel wall. It was suspended from another small metal cable. Knowing that this was a very old Spanish mine, I realized I was looking at an antique object that the brave Spaniards had used for descending into this bottomless pit. The thought that anyone would get into that open bucket and, hanging by little more than a heavy wire, be let down several thousand feet by a windlass struck me with horror.

As I stood there thinking of the recklessness of those old Spaniards, there arrived silently from above, stopping on a level with us, an object which at first seemed vaguely familiar and then all of a sudden shockingly recognizable. It was a perfect replica of that old bucket—and we were expected to descend in it.

The engineer reached out and pulled the bucket over to the edge of the vertical hole, next to where we were standing. When he had done that, Eileen, to my amazement, sprang into it. Lowelito appeared to hang back a moment, but I knew he would enter, for his faith in people was boundless. Like Eileen he carried his brightly burning lamp. Now it was my turn, but I had frozen several feet from the edge of the hole. The young engineer turned to me and made a polite gesture, indicating that I was to precede him while he held the bucket against the edge for me. Having lived in Mexico off and on for a long time, I now made the mistake of behaving in the best Mexican tradition.

"*Después de usted, señor,*" I said. ("After you, sir.")

The usual polite play followed, and in the end the engineer entered the bucket ahead of me.

What followed can only be described as gruesome. Cautiously approaching that hole, I saw that it became lost in darkness below. I also saw that the bucket was now not only well filled, but swinging several feet out, and that I, the polite one, would have to step across to it and enter among all those flames which the bucket riders dangled down at their sides. I finally got my courage and stepped across, getting one foot in the bucket and one hand on the bucket rim. Then I did the splits as the bucket swung outward. But in such a situation a person always has superhuman strength, and I pulled myself safely into the bucket. I did, however, leave my own lamp burning brightly on the edge of the horizontal tunnel.

It took a long time for the windlass to let us down two thousand feet. Considering the character of the bucket, I tried not to imagine the nature of the windlass above, but that was impossible. I kept visualizing a couple of carefree Indians up there laboriously turning an old, rusty iron handle stuck into a log whose ends were resting in two tree forks.

As we descended, we passed several tunnels leading off from the vertical hole, and when finally we came to a halt, we were on the level of a tunnel. The bucket was turned so that I was facing into this tunnel as we came to rest on a wooden platform. I could see at the entrance a shrine decorated with paper flowers and a picture of the Virgin of Guadalupe. Below us I could see a body of dark water that had flooded all the lowest levels.

After the engineer, Eileen and I stepped out of the bucket onto the solid platform, but when I looked back Lowelito on all fours was climbing along a pole that led to the opposite side of the vertical tunnel. The beams on that side had not been covered with planks, and there was Lowelito crawling along like a raccoon and balancing above the dark water far below. Apparently he believed we were following him. When I yelled at him, he saw his mistake and managed to make a dangerous U-turn and join the rest of us.

What we found down in those dark passageways after we had passed the beautiful shrine to the Virgin was continuously exciting, but during all the time I was down there I could not rid my mind of the thought that there would be no stairway available when the time came to ascend. Either we would remain down there forever, or else we would be lifted in that same old bucket by those same carefree, tequila-drinking Indians on top of the mountain.

In the end, of course, we did make the ascent. We were all carried ever so slowly upward, but eventually we were again on top of the earth and out in the white sunlight.

For whatever it was worth, Eileen, Lowelito, and I could now say that we had been down into a very old and deep mine in Guanajuato. And Lowelito and I could add that when finally we were able to introduce Guanajuato to Eileen, she introduced it to us instead, in a most unexpected and unforgettable way.

CHAPTER SEVEN

Tenayuca and the Tlaloc of Coatlinchan

Perhaps it was because Eileen had found two new friends who enjoyed camping in Baja as much as we did that the time seemed to pass so rapidly after our last trip to the mainland of Mexico. It was fortunate that she had found those camping friends, for Lowelito, our usual camping companion, suddenly quit his college job and moved to Virginia. He had discovered that something was wrong with his heart, and his wealthy brother, the chairman of the board of Sears Roebuck, persuaded him to resign from the college and move to the manor house on a large plantation his brother owned in Virginia. Eileen and I were greatly disappointed by this development, and we were worried about Lowelito's health.

We started going to Baja with these new friends. Almost every weekend we went with them to some place below the border. We took them to see the big sycamore tree where Lowelito had buried his hammock, we took them to Table Mountain, and on one occasion, during a Mexican election day, we introduced them to Tequila Springs.

It had long been our custom, when Lowelito was along, to bury any liquor left over from our camps. We did this for several reasons. One was that it was against the law to take liquor back across the border. Another reason was that the liquor would be available whenever we returned to that place. Still another reason, according to Lowelito, was that when we were back home and started thinking of that buried liquor, we would decide to go on another camping trip into Baja.

On this occasion with our new friends, it was an election day. Suddenly Mr. Robert Thompson, one of our new friends, said excitedly, "We don't have any rum, and all the liquor stores are closed!"

His wife, LaRue, the other new friend, said to him, "Robert, if you knew it was election day in Mexico, why didn't you bring some liquor from home? The Mexicans don't care if you bring liquor across the border."

"Everardo should have brought some," Eileen chimed in. She even suggested that we go back across the border for liquor.

None of us drank much, but we did not like the idea of being completely out of rum. Lowelito had shown us many times how important it was to have liquor to offer any Mexican "who might be doing us a favor."

At that point I said, "Don't you worry. We'll go over and get some liquor at Tequila Springs. Eileen, you know very well that the liquor stores never close at that place."

So having assured them that I could get a supply of liquor for the trip, I turned off the main road onto a narrow dirt road that led over to the ocean, just a mile or so to the west.

"This area along here is called Tequila Springs," I said to Don Roberto. There being no house in sight, let alone a liquor store, he looked puzzled. I stopped the car near the beach and told him to bring a shovel and come with me. Walking over to a certain spot where a clump of bushes was sticking up out of the sand and where someone had dumped a pile of old rusty cans, I moved some of the cans to one side with my foot and said to Don Roberto, "Dig here."

When he began to dig furiously, I warned him to dig slowly and carefully. Soon, to his amazement, he began to uncover the liquor Eileen, Lowelito, and I had buried at that spot. He uncov-

ered four or five bottles of Bohemia beer, several bottles of tequila, and two one-gallon jugs of rum.

"Well, you were right; this really is Tequila Springs," Roberto
said happily.

.   .   .

Since returning with Eileen and Lowelito from Guanajuato, I
had become very busy making illustrations for a book to be pub-
lished by the Heritage Press and also by the Limited Editions Club
of New York. The book was *The Conquest of Peru*, by William
Hickling Prescott. The publisher, Mr. George Macy, had asked
me to do the illustrations for the new edition he was to bring out.
Just before our trip to Baja with the Thompsons, I had finished
the illustrations and had sent them in, and now I had almost forgotten about them.

But when we returned from that Baja trip, I found a telegram
waiting for me, requesting that I go immediately to Mexico City
to supervise the color-printing of my illustrations and to autograph
all the Limited Editions Club books. These books were to be printed
and bound in the Imprinta Nuevo Mundo, a print shop in the
village of Tlalpam, a suburb of Mexico City.

I saw this assignment in Tlalpam as an opportunity to visit two
pre-Columbian monuments that I considered important because
of my college course. One was the old Chichimec pyramid of Tenayuca, just outside Mexico City. The other was an ancient and unfinished statue of the rain god Tlaloc, which lay on its back attached to the native rock up a canyon somewhere near the village
of Coatlinchán, a few miles from Texcoco.

As I left Mexico City for Tlalpam, I kept thinking of those two
pre-Columbian sites. Wanting to see them as soon as possible, I
was eager to get done with signing the books and choosing the
colors for the printer. I worked as fast as I could that day, and
finally my assignment in Tlalpam was finished. Now I was ready
to go to Tenayuca. I had decided to go there first, because I was
not at all sure I would ever find the old Tlaloc of Coatlinchán.

Early the next morning, I went to the west side of the National
Palace in Mexico City, from which place buses marked "Tlalne-

pantla por San Bartolo" would run very close to the village of Tenayuca.

When I entered the bus, I saw at once that there were no Indians on board. The bus was filled with mestizos, all men, and among them was a policeman who had a big pistol on his hip, a club dangling from his wrist, and a bulky guitar hanging by a strap over his shoulder.

Before taking a seat, I spoke to the bus driver, telling him that I wanted to go to Tenayuca to see the old pyramid and that I would appreciate his kindness if he would let me know where to get off. The policeman overheard this conversation. Shifting his guitar around in front so that he could sit next to me, he said, "Señor, with your permission, I would like to accompany you to the pyramid of Tenayuca. There are some bad characters in that village."

Although I would have preferred being alone, I considered it an extraordinary honor to have along a man so well equipped for any emergency. I thanked him and said that I would be very pleased to have him visit the pyramid with me.

After a pleasant morning bus ride through the adobe-lined streets and on out Calzada Vallejo into the countryside, the bus driver stopped and let the policeman and me off at the San Bartolo Bridge. Soon I was walking into the village of Tenayuca alongside a man who apparently had two professions, musician and warrior. I knew that people had been living at this place continuously for at least nine hundred years, and that the houses I was seeing had been built upon other houses, which in turn had been built upon still other houses, for many generations, until finally a point in the distant past could be reached when the houses were those of a people who only recently had begun living a sedentary life. They were the Chichimecas. I was also thinking that had I been here at that time, I might have been walking along with a warrior who was dressed in the skin of a jaguar and carrying a bow and arrows.

We were now walking on an unpaved dirt street that ran between unpainted adobe houses from whose walls most of the plaster had fallen. The sidewalk was too narrow for two people to walk abreast on it, and besides, it was cluttered with dogs. The dogs also were mixed breeds, although I doubted if they had any of the genes of the dogs kept by the ancient Chichimecas, who considered dogs a favorite food.

Continuing along this street, which had a solid wall of adobe houses on each side, we soon arrived at an intersection, and there before us, only a few paces away, was the ancient pyramid of Tenayuca.

This, I knew, was an Aztec structure. The Chichimecas had built one pyramid over the other every fifty-two years, and when the Aztecs became the dominant tribe in the valley they continued this practice themselves, building their own pyramids over those of the Chichimecas. I was glad to see this Aztec pyramid, even though it covered up the work of the Chichimecas, for I was not too familiar with Aztec art.

My friend the policeman and I were especially interested in the wall of stone snakes on the pyramid platform. This snake wall extended around three sides of the pyramid, with all the snakes, side by side, projecting outward until their heads extended over the edge of the platform. It occurred to me that the expression on the faces of these serpents probably revealed the spirit of Aztec form at Tenayuca. The single word best describing that expression would be "snarl," for snarling is what those snakes were doing, as though daring anyone to come within their reach.

We decided to count the snakes, but first the policeman placed his guitar on the head of one of the snakes so that he would know where his count began. When he looked around and saw his guitar over that terrible snarling snake, he turned back, removed the guitar, and placed it on the ground in front of the snake.

"What's the matter?" I asked him. "Do you think the snake will bite your guitar?"

"Señor," he answered, "who knows? These snakes are not dead, even though they are made of stone and *mezcla* [mortar]."

I agreed with him completely. It seemed to me amazing that I could see those objects, not as so much stone and cement, but as alive and menacing. I even imagined that if I were to break one open I would find inside all the organs of a snake.

I had read that there were fifty-two snakes on each side, a number representing the cycle of years at the end of which, if the world did not come to an end, the pyramid would be enlarged. Begin-

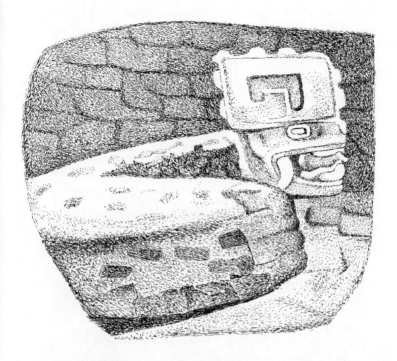

ning our count at the policeman's guitar, I went in one direction, and he the other. When we returned and compared our numbers, I had a total of one hundred forty snakes, while his count was one hundred forty-one. The policeman started counting all over again. When he came back around to the guitar, he was laughing.

"Señor," he said, "this time I found only one hundred thirty-nine snakes. Two of those snakes moved around to the other side while I was counting!"

He wanted to start counting all over again, but I told him it didn't matter, that he had discovered something far more important, which was that the snakes were alive.

The policeman's presence had not interfered at all with my seeing and drawing that day. Despite the arrival of a group of tourists, whose members took no great interest in the pyramid and therefore remained only a few minutes, I was able to make a number of drawings. My visit had been most interesting and profitable.

Now I was on speaking terms with Aztec art. The sun was low in the west, lighting with its red rays the great double stairway that led steeply up to where the twin temples had stood in ancient times. The policeman and I had become good friends. We shook hands, wishing that we both would travel with God. He then departed in the direction of the village, and I walked toward the San Bartolo Bridge, where the bus would pass. As I walked away,

I heard the policeman strumming his guitar. Looking around, I could see him in the distance with his back to me as he walked away. I could also see his big *pistola* bouncing up and down as he stroked his guitar.

.   .   .

There now remained only my visit to the great Tlaloc of Coatlinchán before I would be ready to return to California. I had never seen even a photograph of that pre-Columbian god of rain and

thunder, but I knew it was near the ancient village of Coatlinchán, and that it was the largest piece of stone sculpture ever carved
in the round in the Western Hemisphere. I also knew that it was
still attached to the native rock from which it had been carved
more than a thousand years ago.

Because the great statue had been abandoned before its completion and never disconnected from the matrix rock, some schol-
ars have said that it symbolized the downfall of the ancient civi-
lization, which lacked the will to complete it. But because it was
abandoned in the very early period of Teotihuacán, and because
development was to continue there for many centuries, this does
not seem to me to explain its unfinished state. After the destruc-
tion of Tenochtitlán, the Aztec capital, the Indians attributed
Tlaloc's location and supine position to the Spaniards. Their story
was that the Spaniards, who had demonstrated their outstanding
ability to topple Aztec statues from the summits of pyramids, had
found this great stone figure standing on top of a mountain and
had tossed it several miles into the canyon, where now it was lying on its back.

How to get to the statue was my first problem. I knew it was
in a canyon near Coatlinchán, and because Coatlinchán is itself
located only a few miles from the old city of Texcoco, I decided
that that was where I should begin my search. So I caught a bus
which had a sign in front with the name "Texcoco."

Skirting the white salt flats left after the Spaniards had drained
the lake, the bus arrived at the main plaza of Texcoco, a town which
impressed me as being gray, dusty, and neglected, despite its important place in the history of the Valley of Mexico. A number
of old, dust-covered taxicabs were parked along one side of the
square plaza. Facing the bandstand in the center of the plaza, they
reminded me of a family of pigs nursing an old sow. I looked the
cabs over and found one which appeared a bit more trustworthy
than the others. A small boy was standing nearby, and I said to
him, "*Joven ¿quién es el dueño de este vehículo? ¿Puedes encon-
trarle, por favor?*" ("Young man, who is the owner of this vehicle?
Can you locate him, please?")

The little boy, dressed in dirty white clothes, dashed away. Almost immediately he came back with the driver of the taxi, who

looked even more soiled than his automobile. You could tell, though, that his dirty shirt had once been very white. There were no buttons on the sleeves, and they flapped about his dark wrists. He wore jet-black pants, so dusty that I imagined he must have been lying on the ground working beneath his car.

"Señor," I asked, "does this fine automobile belong to you? I want to go to Coatlinchán, and I was hoping that I might be carried there in such a sturdy-looking car as this."

The man appeared to be very eager, and he answered, "Señor, with much pleasure I can transport you to that village, if only you will pay me in advance so that I can buy gasoline."

The deal was closed, and we were off around the block to a place where gasoline was sold from a metal barrel. Then we headed southward from Texcoco in a cloud of dust churned up by the taxi-cab's well-worn, underinflated tires. I had chosen to ride in the back seat, because the upholstery in the front seat next to the driver was badly torn. As we moved along the dirt road at breakneck speed, which I had expected, I said a silent prayer to Tlaloc. I asked him to please guide me to his great stone likeness.

The distance to Coatlinchán from Texcoco is not more than eight miles, so despite the bad road we arrived soon. But the road we had traveled was like a smooth pavement compared to the streets of Coatlinchán. They were so broken and full of deep holes that the driver had to reduce his speed to about two miles per hour.

The houses on either side of the village street were made of sun-dried adobe bricks of a dead-gray color. If there ever was any plaster over the bricks, it had long since fallen away. I was pleased to be in the streets of Coatlinchán, the "Place of the Snake," and I asked the driver to take me to where we could get directions to the great stone Tlaloc.

Eventually we arrived before an adobe building exactly like all the others we had passed along the street. This building had an open doorway around which people were gathered. The street at this point had taken a dive downward, so the narrow sidewalk in front of the doorway was at least eight feet above the level of our taxicab. All the people around the doorway looked like Indians, but I felt sure they could speak Spanish.

I got out of the cab, climbed up to the doorway, and passed

through it into a surprisingly small, dark room. As soon as my eyesight became adjusted, I saw that I was in a store, where cheese, rope, and tequila were for sale. Behind the counter, which was no more than five feet back from the doorway, stood a man in white *calzones* with a large straw hat on his head. In a dark corner to his left sat an Indian woman. Above her head were shelves loaded with tequila bottles, and hanging on the wall behind the man was a row of machetes, their gray blades looking sharp. Long strips of old flypaper hung from the ceiling rafters. No other people were in the store, for there was so little room. If a person wanted to buy something in that place, he should buy it and then get outside so that someone else could come in and make a purchase.

I stepped up to the counter and said, "*Perdóneme, señor,* I have come here to see the great stone figure of Tlaloc, which I was told is nearby. The driver of the car outside will take me there if you will kindly tell me the route we should follow."

To my surprise, the man behind the counter looked very startled and began to call out in a frightened voice, "*¡José! ¡José! ¡Ven acá!*"

Immediately another man came through the doorway, followed by a boy in a blue shirt. This man seemed eager to be of service. "*¿Puedo ayudarle en algo, señor?*" he asked. ("Can I help you in any way, sir?")

When I explained to him that I wanted to go to the Tlaloc of Coatlinchán and hoped that he could direct me, he replied, "Señor, you follow this street and soon you will enter a lane bordered by rock fences on both sides. You should continue in that lane until it comes to an end. This you can do in the car. From that point on you will have to walk, and I cannot tell you how to go from there. It will be necessary to have a person walk with you who knows the trail. This boy knows that trail, and he will be pleased to go with you."

I thanked the man, José, and also the man behind the counter. The Indian woman had not moved during our conversation. She had not even looked in our direction, so I did not speak to her. The boy in the blue shirt then followed me down the embankment to the car, where we found the driver sound asleep behind the steering wheel. I awakened him and told him to proceed "*de-*

recho, derecho hasta la terminación del camino" ("straight ahead to the end of the road"). He looked puzzled but asked no questions. We were now off again. After only a few hundred yards we entered the stone-fence-bordered lane, which we followed to its end, about two miles away. From that point, we would have to walk. The little boy assured me that the distance was not great.

I now explained to the driver, "We are going to walk from here to the Tlaloc. Park your car right here. If you have not seen that great monument, you will want to come along with us."

"Señor," he answered, "I have not seen that idol, and I have been told that it has great magic, but with your permission I shall wait here in my car. I have no desire to see that idol and would much prefer to sleep here until you return."

The boy and I took off down a narrow trail through a pasture covered with dry grass and weeds. Here and there in the pasture, a few mesquite trees were growing. This being December, the middle of the dry season on the Mexican Plateau, the country everywhere around was parched.

Ahead of us, beyond the pasture, was a stretch of low rolling hills of a reddish color on which there appeared to be no vegetation at all, just dirt and rocks. The shadows, however, indicated that there were canyons or arroyos within that area, and I knew there was no way to tell from a distance how deep they were.

The little boy was leading the way. Soon he motioned to me that we would leave the dirt trail, and then he turned off to the left. After a few steps we climbed into an ancient aqueduct, which was bone dry. It was about three feet wide inside, with stone sides two or three feet high. It was easy to walk in this trough, which sloped gently downward as we proceeded westward. After about a half-mile, the aqueduct crossed a deep arroyo, the old structure held up by graceful arches set upon tall stone columns.

As we entered this part, the little boy pointed to a block of stone in the aqueduct wall to our left. There, carved into the stone, was a date: 1811. This aqueduct was built, then, during the Spanish colonial period, some ten years before Mexico gained her independence from Spain. Because the sides of the aqueduct were low, it was frightening to look down into the deep arroyo below. It was as though we were crossing that deep crack in the earth on a narrow board. I was thankful for the aqueduct, because the sides of the arroyo were almost vertical, with great boulders jutting out from them. It would have been most difficult to get across by climbing down to the bottom and then climbing up the other side.

After crossing the arroyo, we stepped out of the aqueduct and started walking along another faint trail, up onto one of those low, denuded hills. There was not a sprig of grass nor a weed growing there, only a few cactus plants scattered at intervals. The ground was covered with small volcanic rocks, among which were thousands of pottery shards. I picked up some of the shards and saw that they were all pre-Columbian, fragments of broken pots and bowls. Some had colored designs on them. I felt sure that if I looked carefully I might find a figurine, or at least a little clay head, but I was beginning to get anxious about arriving at the great Tlaloc. The boy had said that it was only a kilometer from the car, and already we had walked over two kilometers. I was beginning to wonder if my little guide was lost. A that point we started down a sloping trail that led into a sandy draw. As we followed this draw, its sides became higher and higher. Then we came into a broad, dry riverbed, with steep cliffs on the far side, and there before my eyes — resting high above the sandy riverbed, like a great stranded ship — was the Tlaloc of Coatlinchán.

How strange and mysterious it appeared, stretched out for about twenty-five feet, flat on its back in this lonely, desolate place. Not a soul was in sight, nor had we seen one person on our walk to this place. Here was perhaps the largest piece of stone sculpture in the round ever carved by man in this hemisphere, a figure abandoned before completion a thousand or more years ago. I could not help wondering how those ancient Texcocanos thought they would transport it to their town, had they ever completed it. It was estimated to weigh three hundred tons.

The native rock to which the statue was attached, and upon which it rested, extended at least six feet above the valley floor. In order to see the figure well, I would have to get on top of it. But to get on top would certainly be difficult; the distance from the riverbed, on which I stood, to the top, or upper surface, was nearly twenty feet, and of course I had no ladder.

The boy and I had the good fortune to find two mesquite limbs of sufficient length. They had been washed downstream and were partly covered with sand. Noticing this, I imagined that there probably had been times when Tlaloc was lying on the sand bed rather than high above it, which would have made working on it less difficult for the sculptors.

My little guide proved to be a typical Mexican genius. He now brought me some short pieces of mesquite wood for the steps of my proposed ladder, and he also brought yards and yards of a strong vine that grew in the sandy riverbed. With these materials we soon had a ladder. Although it was very primitive, it served my purpose, and before long I was standing on top of the great Tlaloc of Coatlinchán, as high as a two-story building.

Walking up and down over Tlaloc's stone image, and looking at the desolate country all around me, and at the sky, I was extremely impressed. Foremost in my mind was a question: Why did these ancient sculptors put down their tools and walk away after they had gone to so much work carving the figure's general proportions?

Being so close to the figure, I could not take it all in at once, but I was able to form a mental image of it as a clearly unified group of geometric blocks. In this sense, the figure might have been considered finished, but in terms of representation much work still had to be done. For example, below the elbows the arms were nothing more than two blocks extending outward.

While looking at those two blocks I recognized what might be the reason that the great figure had been abandoned. To this day I do not know if my theory is valid, but years later I found more evidence to support it. What I noticed was that the left arm appeared to have been broken off at a point which made it much shorter than the right arm. Obviously, the great figure would have had to be reduced in size drastically if both arms were to be carved in the same proportion. Realizing this, the sculptors may have decided to abandon the work altogether.

Such was my excitement at this observation that I even imagined how it might have happened: an Indian apprentice had hit the stone too hard with his stone mallet, breaking off a piece of that left arm. I saw him, in my mind's eyes, calling the master sculptor, who recognized immediately that the figure as planned was ruined beyond repair. I also imagined that the apprentice was grabbed by the hair of his head and sacrificed on that spot to the god of rain and thunder.

Years later I explained my theory about the great Tlaloc to my friend Donal Hord, the sculptor, whose own large stone statue *Water* stands in front of the San Diego County Administration Center. A replica of it stands on the embarcadero in Yokohama, Japan. Donal told me that his own helper had drilled too far into the original block of that statue, which error made it necessary for Donal to reduce by several feet the height he had planned for his figure.

After examining the Tlaloc as carefully as possible from my unusual vantage point, I climbed down my makeshift ladder and drew the great reclining figure as viewed from about two hundred feet away.

The little Mexican boy and I now retraced our steps to the car. We found our driver sleeping so peacefully, with both feet extending out the cab window, that I regretted having to awaken him. My kindly feeling toward him was somewhat dissipated, however, after he had turned his taxicab around and we were on our way back to Coatlinchán. We had not gone over a mile when his car ran out of gasoline!

"Señor," I said, "you will recall that I paid you in advance so that you could buy gasoline. I also went with you to the *gasolinera*, where I assumed that you were putting gasoline into your tank. What has happened? Does your tank have a hole in it?"

"No, señor," he answered, "my gas tank does not leak. It is just that my car has a great appetite for gasoline, the way some men have an appetite for tequila. Señor," he added, "my car is a *verdadero borracho* [a veritable drunkard]. It does not know when to stop drinking gasoline."

On the floor of his cab, he carried a gallon can, which he now removed. He screwed off its top and blew into it. Satisfied that the can was in adequate condition, he started walking down the lane toward the village of Coatlinchán. The distance was only about two kilometers, so he was soon back with the gallon of gasoline, which he poured into the tank. We then drove into the village and quickly reached the place where gasoline was sold. But to my surprise the cabdriver drove right on.

"Señor!" I called. "Are you not going to get more gasoline here?"

"No, señor," he replied, "my car is already so drunk from the gasoline he drank on the road that he will drink very little of this that I have just made available to him. It will carry us to Texcoco."

"No, señor!" I insisted. "You stop your car at this *gasolinera* and I will make you a gift of a tankful of gasoline. I do not want this drunkard of yours to get sober."

He stopped the car and backed up to the gas station. I paid to have his tank filled to overflowing. Now we could start back to the sleepy town of Texcoco with some assurance of arriving there. I paid my little guide for his excellent service, and the driver and I were again moving slowly up and down and sidewise through the tortuous main street of Coatlinchán.

"Let your taxicab get as drunk as he pleases now," I said, "so long as he keeps marching down the road."

When we arrived in Texcoco I took the bus back to Mexico City. My own projects for that Mexico trip having been completed, the next day, I caught an airplane, which carried me in a few hours back to Eileen, in California.

CHAPTER EIGHT

Travels with My Grandsons

During the ten-year period between 1956 and 1966, Eileen and I had gone into Baja California at least twenty-two times. We had also made four long trips to the mainland of Mexico, two of them in a four-wheel-drive truck with camper, which we had acquired in 1958. Now, in 1967, Eileen said that we should give more attention to the education of our grandsons. Stephen and Winthrop had gone with us on countless trips to Baja, but neither of them had set foot on the mainland of Mexico.

"I think it is high time we introduced Stephen to Mexico," she said. "He has had his fifteenth birthday, and I think we should give him a birthday present of a trip with us all over Mexico, in our station wagon. Later, when Winty becomes fifteen, we should do the same for him."

We had had those boys with us so much that when the time came to go on the mainland trip, it seemed absurd that I should have to get a notarized permit from my own daughter before I could take either of her sons down into Mexico.

When we reached the border at San Luis, Sonora, in our station wagon, I presented our papers and the notarized permit to a Mexican border official. Written on the permit was the date of my grandson's birth.

The border official read the permit slowly. I could tell that he was thinking, but for a moment it did not occur to me what he was thinking about. Finally he said to me, "Señor, this document indicates that your grandson had his fifteenth birthday several months ago."

"That is correct," I answered.

"Well, then," he continued, "this document is not the requisite one to permit your grandson's entry into Mexico."

"Why not?" I asked in alarm. I had driven over two hundred miles to get to this border crossing, and now he was suggesting that I might have to go all the way back and start again.

"Your grandson," he replied, "has passed the age of fifteen years, and our Mexican law says that he must get a regular tourist permit to enter Mexico *after* the age of fifteen years."

"But he is still fifteen," I said. "He will not be sixteen for some time. This permit was read and approved by the Mexican consul, Señor Ignacio Pesquiera, in San Diego, California. He is a friend of mine."

The official looked up from the paper he held in his hand and said, "Señor Pesquiera is not a Mexican consul in San Diego, California!"

"Señor," I said, "if Señor Pesquiera is not the Mexican consul in San Diego, then it is strange that he believes he is the consul, and that everyone in San Diego and Tijuana also believes he is the consul. I was in the consul's office just yesterday, and all his secretaries believe he is the consul. I shall inform him that he is mistaken if that is your wish. I can telephone him this surprising information from here in San Luis."

At this point, the official smiled and handed the permit back to me. "Very well," he said, "your grandson can accompany you into Mexico."

I had won a victory, after an argument that I knew very well could have been won in seconds with a five-dollar bill. But the Mexican *mordida* has always been very offensive to me. I have always felt that those Mexicans who practice it are staining the honor of a country I love.

Just outside San Luis, we drove head-on into a sandstorm that was so violent I could not see the narrow pavement ahead of me. I pulled the car over to the right side of the road, and soon the road was completely covered with sand. Eileen put her scarf over her face as we waited for the storm to blow over, but Stephen was so fascinated that he got out of the car and walked out into the whirling yellow sand. The storm was over within less than an hour and we continued on south — our final destination, Mexico City.

Eileen and I wanted our grandson to *live* through Mexico rather than to sleep through it, so when he got out of the car in that sandstorm and became lost from our sight after he had moved only a few yards away, we felt that he would take everything in and not take anything for granted. Although he had been going to school for years, so far he had not been persuaded regarding what he should see, and especially what he should ignore, about the world around him. When we stopped for lunch in the desert and found the heat very unpleasant, we decided to eat our lunch while the motor kept running and the air conditioning was on. Soon, though, the motor became overheated, forcing us to turn it off and with it the cool air. Immediately the character of the place poured in, impressing itself on us clearly and unmistakably. Later we had the good fortune to encounter a rain, a Mexican rain, the kind that must have given birth to the ancient beliefs about the rain gods Tlaloc, on the Mexican Plateau, and Chac, in Yucatán.

It is impossible to know what a Mexican rain is from hearsay. After one has been in such a rain, however, he will know that he has had a new experience. A Mexican rain on the plateau seems to have a definite objective, to soak everything thoroughly. It comes down white and gray-blue from somewhere above. One does not usually look up while it is falling; he looks straight ahead at it. If one is traveling in a car when a Mexican rain begins, he watches it dance and splatter on the ground, forming a lake that soon rises above the highway and hides it. The only thing to do then is stop the car, set the brakes, and wait. The rain may not last long. When it stops, as suddenly as it began, the water usually moves quickly off the pavement. There are times, however, when the accumulation of water from many consecutive rains may put a stop to all transportation. When that occurs, it is better to be a Mexican than a North American, for Mexicans are a part of the rain. They are also a part of the wind, and the sunshine, and of all growing things, and even a part of death.

During that particular rain Stephen must have discovered that what he had experienced formerly had not given him a true understanding of the essential character of rain. From then on, I thought, he would carry in his mind a rain yardstick. To get a thorough knowledge of Mexican rains, though, he would have to see those of Mexico City, those of Jalapa (called *chipichipi*), and those that fall in the rain forests of Mexico's southeast.

As we drove south, we had to remind ourselves from time to time that Mexico City was our destination. Along the way many events distracted us. When we were in the long, narrow street leading through the town of Ixtlán del Río, for example, we met two immense, gray, nude elephants walking rapidly toward us down the street, minding their own business and staying on their side of the narrow roadway.

As the elephants came closer, appearing more tremendous each second, Stephen exclaimed excitedly, "Look at those big elephants coming!"

"I know," I answered; "they must be going home for lunch. This street is so narrow I think I'll stop the car and wait till they get by us."

"Put the windows up!" Eileen shouted.

"They can't get in the windows," I assured her.

"No, but they can get their snouts in!" she answered in alarm.

We held our breath as the huge monsters glided past us without even giving us a sidewise glance. They seemed to know where they were going, even though no human attendant was present to guide them. As soon as the elephants were behind us, I moved rapidly ahead up the street. Stephen, with his knees on the seat, kept looking out the back window until they were lost in the distance.

Thinking that the sight of elephants coming down the street so nonchalantly in a Mexican village might confuse Stephen, I said, "Don't get the idea that you are going to see any more elephants walking about free in the streets of Mexico. That was most unusual. I never saw it before in my forty-five years in Mexico, and you probably will never see it again. Elephants are not native down here, and people don't usually keep them for pets or for work animals."

After having got by the elephants, we continued on through that busy Mexican village of one long street. Ixtlán del Río, in the state of Nayarit, is a tropical place of pretty mango trees, red-tile-roofed houses, bananas, beautiful flowering bushes, and myriads of colorful butterflies.

Just beyond the town, the road curves onto a higher level before continuing southward. Barely a mile out of the town, a small barbed-wire gate may be seen on the left side of the road. Almost immediately inside that gate are the ruins of an ancient pre-Columbian ceremonial center. Perhaps it has not been singled out as a tourist attraction because it doesn't look impressive. A ruin should be quite large and made of very heavy stones — the kind that look as though they could be moved only by modern machinery — to be a good tourist attraction. At this ceremonial center, Stephen and I counted eight low mounds covered with vegetation. One circular stone structure there had two square stone altars on its flat top.

There seemed to me to be an echo of distant Xochicalco in the form of this monument. It made me recall the wind that blows softly over fields of yellow flowers at that place. I knew that the Toltec culture had reached as far as Ixtlán, and I also remembered that Ce Acatl, one of the Toltec rulers, had been raised in Xochicalco, near the modern Mexican city of Cuernavaca.

On our journey from Ixtlán to Mexico City, about the only guiding principle Eileen and I kept in mind was that we were introducing our grandson to Mexico. He was now in a strange land, where he did not know any of the people, and where none of them knew him — or so we thought.

"Are we going through Pátzcuaro?" Stephen asked. "I hope so, because I have some friends there. I know a lot of girls there."

"Okay," I said. "I want to go there anyway, because I want you to meet Marco Polo, in Tzintzuntzan. You don't happen to know the mayor of Pátzcuaro, do you?"

Just how a fifteen-year-old gringo boy who had never been to mainland Mexico could know lots of girls in Pátzcuaro was a mystery to me, but as it turned out he did look those girls up and bring them around for us to meet. He had met them back in the States.

About six years before, Eileen and I had camped for a week up among the *yácatas* (the name that has been given to the truncated pyramids of western Mexico) just above the village of Tzintzuntzan. Bob and LaRue Thompson were with us on that trip. Tzintzuntzan, on Lake Pátzcuaro, had been the capital of the ancient Tarascan nation during the days when the Aztecs dominated the Mexican Plateau and everything else to the east coast and

south to what is now the Guatemalan border. But the Aztecs definitely had not dominated the Tarascans, whose territory covered all of what is now the state of Michoacán.

It was while we were camping above Tzintzuntzan one stormy night that Marco Polo García was born, in a little one-room house made of roughly hewn volcanic stones, with a roof of straw and tile. This low, shedlike house, near which we were camped, was perched on the very edge of the broad *yácata* platform. The next morning, bright and early, after the all-night rain, Alfonso García, the father, who was the official caretaker of the Tarascan ruins, came to tell us the good news. But there was something troubling him, something he wanted to discuss.

"*Señores,*" he began, "my happiness in my new son, who bellows like a bull, has been discouraged by the priest down in the village. I have just been talking with that priest."

"*¿Qué pasó?*" ("What happened?") I asked.

"*Señores*," he continued, "for these past long nine months, during which my son was getting ready for this world, I have been happy to know that it was my privilege to give him the name Marco Polo. It is the name of that famous traveler, whose book I have read over and over again. But the priest down in the village has it in his mind that I should not name my son Marco Polo. Even though there was a Saint Marco, the priest is still opposed to the name Marco Polo for my son."

Eileen's experience covering superior court for her newspaper enabled her to come forward with a solution. She had served as a witness to many weddings in the civil court, weddings which did not make use of clergymen or priests, so she said to Don Alfonso, "Why don't you register your son's name with the civil authorities as Marco Polo and let the priest call him whatever he would like?"

Because we left Tzintzuntzan the next day, we did not know how the naming came out. Now, six years later, Eileen and I were back, and we were eager to learn what name the little boy carried.

After a good breakfast of *pescado blanco* at our hotel in Pátzcuaro, we had driven to Tzintzuntzan for the day. We wanted to go up to the ruins and let Stephen climb over the *yácatas*, and we also wanted to call on Don Alfonso and see his child.

Arriving in the village, I drove our station wagon right up to the gateway to the atrium of the sixteenth-century church. Our car had not come to a complete halt when we were attacked by a squirming, chattering army of little Indian children of all sizes. Getting out of the car, I said to them, "*Buenos días, amiguitos. Estoy aquí en busca de un muchacho que se llama Marco Polo. ¿Conocen ustedes ese muchacho?*" ("Good morning, little friends. I am here in search of a boy named Marco Polo. Do you know that boy?")

These words sent the children into a state of near frenzy. They began to run in all directions, out into the street and around the corner, yelling, "*¡Marco Polo! ¡Marco Polo!*" In no time at all, they converged upon me again, pushing and shoving and pulling along a little six-year-old boy who appeared completely bewildered.

"*¡Aquí está Marco! ¡Aquí está Marco Polo!*" they shouted.

Eileen and I were delighted to see this little boy. Putting my hand on his shoulder, I said to him, "Marco Polo, at last I find you, after six years. Here is a little present for you. I want you to do me a favor to stand guard over my car while I visit the church and the cathedral. Later perhaps you will go with us to see your father. Marco Polo, this is my wife, who helped give you the name Marco Polo, and this is my grandson, Esteban."

Neither Marco Polo nor his young companions knew why he had been singled out among all the rest, but he accepted his assignment very seriously. Taking up a position near the front of the car, he made it obvious that no one had better touch our station wagon while he was on guard over it.

Eileen and I did not know at the time that we would see Marco Polo every two or three years after that visit. The last time we saw him, he was sixteen years old and in secondary school. On that occasion, he escorted Eileen up to the ruins and would not leave her side.

"Marco Polo," Eileen said to him, "I hope you are planning to enter the University of Morelia when you finish *secundaria*. We would be proud if you began studying in the university. A person with so distinguished a name as Marco Polo should not be content with an ordinary life."

Marco looked at Eileen as though he adored her. He handed her a bouquet of four-leaf clovers he had picked among the *yácatas*.

"I want to continue studying," he said, "but I also believe I should travel. I have many desires to travel all the way to Chicago!"

. . .

When Eileen and I arrived in Mexico City with Stephen, we were alarmed at the way progress had hit that ancient place. Buildings with surfaces of glass and shiny marble had shot up here and there like tall weeds in an old, neglected garden. I had the feeling that new tenants had moved in, tenants who had no interest in or love for the old garden. As I saw more of the old buildings surrounding the new ones, though, it became clear that the newcomers had only established a kind of beachhead, that they had not yet become masters of the place. Nevertheless, I had an uneasy feeling that the people I would now encounter in Mexico City would not be like those I had known before. I did notice that drivers were

still in a great hurry, but the number of cars seemed to have increased tenfold. The fast automobiles filled the streets in such a
way as to form several lanes, wherever the width of a street would
permit. I could see no dividing lines, even where there was two-
way traffic.

At one point in this mad traffic, I found myself in the far-right
lane of a street when Stephen, who carried the unfolded map in
his hands, suddenly announced that if I wanted to go to the Hotel
Cortés, I would have to make a left turn at the next corner. Fortunately, a policeman was stationed there in the middle of the mass
of cars. I stopped in my tracks while cars rushed past me on both
sides, and I waved frantically to the policeman. I was praying he
would be one of the old-time Mexicans. He saw me, blew his
whistle, and brought the whole throbbing herd to a dead halt.
He came over to me, and I saw that he had the look of the Mexicans I had known before all this progress had set in.

"Señor," I said, "I hope you will pardon me and not throw us
into prison for stopping, but I have just arrived in your city, and
to get to where I must go I should make a left turn at this very
street corner."

The officer smiled and said, "That is no problem. You should
start turning now, while I hold up the traffic."

I thanked him and added that it was typical for Mexicans to
solve the problems of those who are confused. I made a wide turn
to the left from three lanes over, while hundreds of racing motors
waited until I got around. The officer then blew his whistle again,
and the race went ahead as before. My conclusion was that if the
new people were like this man, we were going to get along fine
together.

Just how it comes about that the attitudes of one generation
are passed on to the next, regardless of new ideas and even new
genes, is a mystery, but that happens often in Mexico. The culture
there could only have sprung from Spanish people and Indian people, but it is itself neither Spanish nor Indian. It is a very strong,
living spiritual entity, having its own characteristics, and the behavior of that policeman was an expression of it. One of those
characteristics is certainly that rules do not come first, that they
do not cover all situations, and that it is up to the one in charge

to solve a problem on his own when no proper rule is at hand.

"Eileen," I said, "one of the first things I want to do after we get settled in our hotel is to take you and Stevie out to Coatlinchán to see that old Tlaloc lying on his back there. That will take a whole day, but I know you will think it is worthwhile."

"Let's go first to the museum," Eileen said, "and let Stevie see the great sculpture of pre-Columbian Mexico. He ought to see the beautiful museum itself."

That seemed sensible to me. In the Museum of Anthropology and Archaeology one can very quickly get an overall idea of the many Indian cultures that preceded the arrival of the Spaniards in Mexico. After a visit there, Stephen would have a better appreciation of that statue of Tlaloc up the canyon beyond Coatlinchán.

So the next day we went out the Paseo de la Reforma, that beautiful avenue Maximilian had ordered built when he was Emperor of Mexico. We arrived at Chapultepec Park and walked immediately to the museum. And there in front of it, standing like a great Japanese temple guardian — and upright — was my old friend the Tlaloc of Coatlinchán, upon whose hard stone belly I had walked back and forth when he lay on his back up that lonely canyon.

Since I had seen that stone figure only when it was in a supine position, it now seemed to me strange that I recognized it the instant my eyes fell upon it. Apparently we do not have to see an object from all angles in order to know how it will appear when seen from any angle. The image that forms in our mind, regardless of what we actually see, must be all-embracing. I now realized, without any doubt, that I was confronted by the great Tlaloc of Coatlinchán, that he had somehow got up on his feet after some sixteen hundred years and reached this new location, despite his weight. Another thought that flashed into my mind as I stood staring was that Eileen had been right when she often chided me for not reading the newspapers and keeping informed about what was happening in the world. The moving of that pre-Columbian figure was a gigantic feat, and the newspapers must have been full of stories about it.

Anyway, here that rain god was, in his great unfinished effigy, and I felt that it was up to me to take advantage of his new posi-

tion and make drawings to discover the precise nature of both his form and his spirit.

As I contemplated him in this position — surrounded by the tall trees of the park, seen against a background of museum walls, and with modern mestizo people on all sides — I suddenly visualized him standing in this same upright position out in the desolate canyon beyond Coatlinchán. With that image in mind, and while my eyes were focused upon him here in the park, it seemed to me that he had taken on a new expression, that he was now in a fury because he had been moved in both time and space. It seemed to me that I heard him mumbling to himself, "Look what has happened! They have transported me to Grasshopper Hill, where those narrow-minded, fanatical Aztecs camped a thousand years after my creation in stone!"

.   .   .

Like most tourists in Mexico City, Stephen was eager to see "the Pyramids." Despite the fact that pyramids exist all over Mexico and Central America, that is the popular name for the ancient ruins of Teotihuacán. Eileen and I wanted to visit Teotihuacán again; we had not been there for many years. I particularly wanted to check on the relation between the form and expression of the old Texcoco statue and that of the art at Teotihuacán.

We decided to go by bus. The one we took was quite elegant, and it was filled with American tourists, who were speaking English on all sides of us. Across the aisle from me, seated next to Stephen, was a middle-aged man who said he taught physical education in high school.

"This is my first visit to these pyramids," he began. "In fact, this is my first trip to Mexico. Have you been here before?"

I said that I had, and that my wife and I were introducing our grandson to Mexico. He told me that he coached the football team at his school and that he wished he could give his team an Indian name. "There is a college football team in California called the Aztecs," he said.

I suggested that there were lots of Indian names available.

"You might call your team the Chichimecas or the Tarascans," I said. "The Tarascans, of Western Mexico, were never defeated by the Aztecs."

He said he liked the name Chichimecas but that he doubted if many people had ever heard of it.

When the bus stopped to let the passengers off, it was so close to the great Pyramid of the Sun that we had to look up, and then up again, in order to take it in. The pyramid's awesome size made everything around it seem small, as it held back all the surrounding space and pushed itself upward toward the sky. The tourists slid silently out of the bus. Immediately, as they scampered about, they seemed to be reduced to the size of ants. I was caught up in this strange world, which has no limits in space and time, when suddenly, from out of my own world, came these words: "Boy, oh boy! Let's go climb it!" Stephen had brought me out of my trance.

We had to walk what seemed an endless distance to get around to where the great stairway led steeply up the face of the pyramid. In 1926, Eileen had climbed those steps in spite of a fever.

"Are you going to do it again?" I asked her. I need not have asked, for I knew Eileen would climb anything that had steps. She would also climb volcanos, but not trees.

Eileen now answered my question by starting up the stone stairway. Looking up the pyramid face would have been like looking down a long railroad track, where the rails appear to converge in the distance, had it not been for the tourists scattered all the way from the base of the pyramid to the top. They had lost no time in scampering up the pyramid's stairway. Stephen was among them. I could see him passing the other climbers one by one.

On our way up I stayed with Eileen, despite the fact that her climbing ability exceeded my own. I felt thankful that she was willing to stop and breathe a moment with me as we reached the summit of each pyramid section.

Stephen had been on the top platform long enough to become acquainted with everybody by the time Eileen and I pulled ourselves onto the topmost step. Other tourists were close behind us, and within a short time the whole group was on top. Now it was like a cocktail party back in the States, except for one thing: everybody was quiet. Nobody was talking. Everyone was quite out of breath.

The entire valley stretched out before our eyes. We were seeing, from our high position, two hundred and ten feet above the valley floor, just what the ancient Teotihuacanos had seen. I knew that our thoughts and feelings could not be the same as theirs, especially since our reasons for climbing the pyramid were not the same as theirs had been. They had climbed as priests in a religious ceremony, perhaps accompanied by captives who would be sacrificed on the stone altar and later thrown down the face of the pyramid. We, on the other hand, had come up for reasons which perhaps a psychologist or a sociologist could best explain. As we stood there, looking down on the valley below, I wondered what Stephen was thinking. I found out soon enough. Suddenly he stepped out of the crowd to the edge of the platform and got the attention of the entire tourist group.

"This is my grandmother who has climbed up here!" he exclaimed. "I'll bet she's the oldest woman on top of this pyramid!"

.   .   .

After our trip with Stephen, which lasted well over a month, we returned to California realizing that Winty's time was next. Almost before we knew it, we saw his fifteenth birthday just ahead of us. So we got a notarized permit from his mother and started to Mexico again, in the summer of 1968. Forty-two years had gone by since Eileen first went to Mexico with me.

On this trip, with our younger grandson, we changed our itinerary. We did not go to Mexico City, but rented the charming old Witter Bynner house right in the center of the village of Chapala. It had become the property of Peter Hurd, the artist, and its caretaker was Remigio Pulido, the son of our old friend Isidoro, who was now dead. Remigio continued to live in Isidoro's house, which adjoined Peter Hurd's house, on Niños Héroes Street. From our rented house we were able to make trips with Winty into other parts of Mexico, although he would have been content to remain in Chapala, where he could ride horses and shoot off fireworks.

During the time we were renting the Witter Bynner house, some sort of feud was going on between Remigio's family and the people who owned the corner grocery store. The grocery-store people served as agents for Peter Hurd. I assumed that they might have been involved in his purchase of the Witter Bynner house, for when foreigners buy property in Mexico it must be done in a roundabout manner. Because of Remigio's feud with them, my guess was that the grocery-store people were lusting for eventual ownership of the property. Perhaps they realized that the members of Isidoro's family had lived on the property so long they might fall heir to it as squatters. The grocery-store people had walled up the doorway that led into our house from the caretaker's house, so Remigio's wife, who was our cook, had to go all around the block each day to enter our house by way of the front door. And because the grocery-store people had put on a lock to which Remigio's wife had no key, we had to let her in each morning. Remigio had not continued his father's tradition of making pre-Columbian art. He did not know how to do that. He did, however, know all the recipes Isidoro had used for making candy, and he continued to make candy in the patio of the caretaker's house, just as Isidoro had done for years.

One day, upon leaving for a three-day trip with Winty over to Pátzcuaro, in the state of Michoacán, I gave our front-door key to Remigio's wife, so that she could get in and clean the house. I never knew for sure why it happened, but when we returned we found that the grocery-store people had put an entirely different lock on the front door. Now, not only the cook was locked out, but so were we. Perhaps the grocery-store people had thought we were not coming back?

At age fifteen Winty was an excellent climber, despite his six feet of thin length. So we went around into the patio of Remigio's house, and I showed Winty how he might scale a wall, climb over the straw roof of a shed, and get into our upper-story dining room, which was open on one side. Once there, he could go down the stairs and unlock the front door.

While Winty was on his way up the wall, I noticed that he had picked up a Mexican companion. They were now helping each other up. Winty was stepping on the Mexican boy's shoulder. When he got onto the roof, he reached down and pulled his companion up with him. I was watching them proceed slowly over the straw roof when suddenly the roof gave way and they both disappeared into whatever room was below.

I yelled at them, "Are you hurt?"

They were laughing down inside the shed. "No, we're not hurt," Winty answered. "This room has a door that leads into the kitchen. I think it's a pantry." Soon they had gone to the front door, unlocked it, and let us in.

The next day, I took the lock off the door and had another one with a different key put on, so that the grocery-store people would be out of our lives. All we had to do now was fix the straw roof, which proved to be easy.

We always called the house "the Witter Bynner house" because that American poet made it so beautiful and so full of surprises while he was living in it. He had come to Chapala with D. H. Lawrence in the early 1920's.

One day, when the toilet facilities in the house had become extremely sluggish, we called in a plumber, who dug a deep trench in our inside patio. Suddenly he climbed up out of the trench in alarm and fled. At the bottom of the trench he had uncovered a skeleton. The bones were almost chalk white, and because a small grinding stone and a *metate* had been buried with the figure, I imagined that the burial had taken place in pre-Columbian times, long before our rented house had been built over the grave. The plumber rushed directly to a cantina and got drunk as fast as possible. We could not get him back on the job for nearly a week because of his drunken condition. When he did return, he had two helpers with him. The two young helpers looked down into the trench while their boss gave them instructions from a distance. He would not go close to the trench, even though he was still well fortified with tequila. I assured him that the skeleton had been removed and that there was nothing to fear, but he only gave a nervous little laugh and kept saying, *"No me gusta; no me gusta ese muerto."* ("I don't like that dead man.")

Seeing that the plumbing job was not going forward, Eileen said to me, "You know the priest. Why don't you ask him to bring some holy water and sprinkle it down in that hole?"

"I don't know the priest that well," I said, "but maybe Alfredo can get him to do it."

As it turned out, we did not need Alfredo's help. The two Mexican boys finally jumped into the trench and began digging. If they had uncovered another skeleton, at a lower depth, the plumbing job never would have been finished. I was sure of that. It would not have mattered, though; when the boys had repaired what they thought needed repairing and had filled the trench, our two toilets continued to operate sluggishly.

CHAPTER NINE

Palenque Revisited

When I returned from Palenque in 1950, I fully intended to go back there with Eileen very soon. However, for reasons difficult to understand, twenty-three years passed before I could take her with me to that ancient Mayan city. Despite the long lapse of time, I felt sure Palenque would be almost the same. The old ruin had survived the attacks of the jungle for over a thousand years; twenty-three years more would make little difference.

Lowelito had recently passed away from a heart attack back in Virginia. We were shocked at his death but not surprised to learn that he had died with a smile on his face. It now seemed appropriate that we go to a place he had loved so much. We knew we would feel his presence there among the old Palenque ruins, although we realized that he continued to live also in the memories of so many of his devoted students and friends.

We started at last on our Palenque trip in the late fall of 1973, flying first to Mérida, Yucatán. After visiting the Maya-Toltec ruins of Chichén Itzá, where Lowelito had worked five years for the Carnegie Institution, and after seeing Uxmal, Xlapac, deep in the

Yucatán bush, and several other Mayan sites, we continued by second-class bus to the old city of Campeche. There we rented a small bug-shaped Volkswagen and began driving toward Palenque. The car was so small that after we had squeezed into it, only a little space remained for our small amount of luggage.

Eileen has always had the instincts of a pack rat, so the lack of extra space in our Volkswagen was frustrating for her in that it would discourage her tendency to acquire objects. But she is so ingenious that she can find good small things to collect if large ones are out of the question, and among the small things she collected was a beautiful and very fragile bouquet of dried wood roses, which she picked among some old Mayan ruins along the way. In Campeche she found a lot of tortoise-shell jewelry, so small that she could wear it or put it in her purse.

We departed from Campeche early one morning, carrying a lunch basket. In the basket we had some tomatoes, which reminded Eileen that we should buy some salt before we got out of town. We also had bananas, avocados, bread, and a bottle of Mexican wine. I stopped at a little grocery store, and Eileen ran in to get the salt. Very soon she returned and said that she needed my help.

"The man in the store seems amazed that all we want is salt," she told me. "I said to him, '*Señor, quiero comprar sal*,' but he only looked at me and didn't move to get any salt. So I said to him, '*Un momento, voy por me esposo.*'"

When I went into the store, I could see that the man looked bewildered, but in the meantime he had placed a large sack of salt on the counter. The salt was in a coarse, brown cloth sack and must have weighed at least fifty pounds.

"The señora said you wanted salt," the man said to me in Spanish.

"That's right," I answered. "How much is that salt?"

Eileen interrupted. "Oh, no! We could never get that in our car."

Eileen insisted that the groceryman go out with her and look at our Volkswagen. When they came back into the store, the man did not say a word but began climbing a ladder to get to a high shelf. He took down a coil of rope, and with a smile announced that he could tie the salt onto the bumper. He picked up the heavy sack, and with the rope over his arm was about to carry the salt to the Volkswagen when I told him not to. He then set the sack back down onto the counter with a jolt, which caused some of the salt to fall out. I now saw my opportunity to end this business. I asked him for a piece of wrapping paper. This request seemed to confuse him, but he handed me a square of the paper. Holding it in one hand at the edge of the counter, I shoved the spilt salt onto it with the other hand, and then folded the paper up over the salt.

"Señor," I said, "this is all the salt we need. How much is it worth?"

"Oh, señor," he replied, "I cannot sell you that small amount. If you wish to take it, you pay me nothing. I thought you wanted the salt for your cows."

"No," I told him, "we only wanted it for our tomatoes, with our lunch."

We thanked him and shook hands with him, and he wished that we might go with God.

. . .

Soon we were out of Campeche and on the road that leads to Escárcega and on to Palenque. When Eileen and I are traveling together in a car, we try to observe the country we are moving through, but we also do a lot of talking about such things as the table decorations she might use at a Christmas party months ahead and many miles away. As we left Campeche, however, we both had those tomatoes and the salt on our minds. I began talking on that subject.

"Mexican tomatoes in this area," I said, "are a lot better than the tomatoes we have back in California. The reason is that they are not raised scientifically. Science undoubtedly has brought many blessings to mankind, but it has taken the flavor out of tomatoes. And it has done the same to chickens."

Eileen wanted to know just how science had destroyed the flavor of chickens. At this point, I'm afraid, I got a bit carried away by my convictions.

"You ought to know about chickens," I said; "your dad once owned a chicken ranch. Scientifically raised chickens don't taste as good as those which have to make their own living by scratching in the dirt and chasing insects. The same is true of their eggs. The scientific chickens live on board floors up on stilts and never have any dirt to scratch around in. When they lay an egg, they do not consider it a creative act to be proud of. This causes the egg to lack the inner spiritual organization a work of art has. That is why the eggs taste so bad and lack nourishment. In fact, I suspect those eggs are a kind of low-grade poison."

I told Eileen that the real reason for scientific chicken raising was social and economic. "The way our society is today," I said, "things have to be mass-produced, whereas in the past every family had a few chickens for its own use. As a result the chickens had a nice life of their own. What is more, for millions of years the chickens evolved slowly into the birds we know today, not by living up off the ground, constantly in eternal daylight, and having food thrown to them for free, but by having to struggle. They got a lot of fun and excitement out of the struggle, and they always laid very tasty eggs. If man could only adjust his own society in such a way and at such a tempo as not to violate the basic rights of chickens and other animals, everybody would be happier. But instead, we use economics. We follow the advice of economists, even though no two of them ever agree and none of them is interested in the quality of living. No economist gives a damn about whether chickens are happy or not."

"You should start a new school of economics based upon the happiness of chickens," Eileen said. "What do you think ever happened to the chicken that flew out of the airplane over the jungle when you and Lowelito were going to Palenque?"

I said he was a lot better off, whatever happened to him, than those scientifically raised factory-worker chickens, but that probably he was dead by now, it being twenty-three years ago that he made his descent.

"And that is why you are wrong when you say we will stay with Don Ernesto in Palenque," said Eileen. "You told me he was an old man when you and Lowelito stayed at his ranch."

By this time we had passed through the dusty little town of Escárcega, which looked so big on the map. We were now approaching a wide bridge that spanned the Usumacinta River. For me it was a thrill to think I was about to cross that great river—a river that had been an important highway for the ancient Mayan Indians for many centuries. I knew that impressive ruined stone cities could be found along its course farther south: Piedras Negras, Yaxchilán, and even Bonampak, whose mural paintings destroyed the old belief among archaeologists that the Mayan city-states of this area lived in perpetual peace.

As we crossed the toll bridge, we could see a number of hand-hewn canoes anchored to the banks of the wide stream. Cormorants were flying down the river toward the sea.

We continued over the bridge toward Catazaja, where we would turn south and be within just twenty-two miles of Palenque. I almost felt guilty going along so easily. I kept thinking of Graham Greene's miserable journey on a mule close to this route in 1933. Like Lowelito and me some years later, that writer stayed for a while with Don Ernesto at his ranch.

We could see on both sides of the road wide stretches of land which only recently had been hidden from the sun by a dense jungle. It was now called "cleared land." In some places, the tall gray trunks of dead jungle trees were still standing, soon to be cut down and removed. I told Eileen that all this was the result of two things: technological progress, particularly bulldozers, and population explosion. "The sad part of it," I said, "is that, along with the jungle, human values are being destroyed."

We turned south at Catazaja, a most indefinite place, with no center and no visible boundaries. Now we were moving straight down the last stretch of road to Palenque. Soon I noticed that Eileen had begun to examine our lunch basket. It was time to find some shady spot off the road.

We could see a small grove of trees ahead of us, about a mile away. This grove had been left standing when the land all around had been cleared of the jungle. When we arrived we found a small dirt road leading off the pavement and into the shade. Obviously this place had been left undisturbed for travelers.

Eileen got out the lunch basket and spread on a cloth our tomatoes, salt, avocados, and bread, while I opened the bottle of *vino tinto*. The day was only half gone, and we were in no hurry. We admired the rich variety of plants and flowers under the big trees, but did not examine them closely for fear of *garrapachos*, those little insects whose acquaintance we had made in the low bush country of Yucatán. Not one car passed during our lunch, nor did any animal or man go by.

When we were back on the road, going along so easily, I had a gnawing feeling of guilt. When I recognized that this feeling was caused by the ease and comfort with which we were getting to Palenque, I knew that I was still making unconscious comparisons between our journey and the suffering experienced by Stephens and Catherwood and by Graham Greene. With this discovery my guilty feeling vanished, but in its place there arose in my mind the thought of impending trouble. Something told me this trip to Palenque was too good to be true.

Houses now began to appear along the roadside. They were unlike those in the suburbs of the village of Palenque twenty-three years before. Although built mostly of thatch, these looked much larger and sturdier. I knew we must be about to reach Palenque village, but I recognized nothing. Nothing was the way it had been when Lowelito and I landed in a cornfield somewhere around this place. I even wondered what had become of that Indian girl who had walked with us all the way to the village.

While I was thinking of these things and seeing so much that was unrecognizable, our Volkswagen started to cough and lose speed.

"What is the matter with it?" Eileen asked excitedly.

"It's got bronchitis," I replied.

"I knew this would happen," Eileen said. "We'll never get out of this place, even if we ever reach Palenque."

"I think we're already there," I said, "or at least within walking distance. Lowelito and I walked into Palenque, and you and I may have to do it, too."

Looking to the side of the road now and down into a gully filled with large trees, I saw a barber's chair out in the open air. A man with a white rag around his neck was seated in the chair getting a haircut. Just to the left of this open-air barbershop was an outdoor mechanic's shop. I could tell it was a mechanic's place because of several old broken-down automobiles there, including one which was pulled up by a heavy rope to a tree.

I went over to the open-air mechanic and said, "*Señor, mi carro de repente no quiere caminar.*" ("Sir, my car suddenly does not want to go down the road.")

The mechanic followed me to our Volkswagen, raised the engine cover, and asked me to start the car. When I did, the motor immediately began to cough and miss badly.

"Ah," he said, "you have a decomposed *bovina.* You must get a new or rebuilt *bovina.* There is one in Emiliano Zapata, which is thirty miles away, and maybe there is one also in that station back down the road, which you can see from here, the one with the banana trees in front."

When he said we needed a new *bovina,* I took his word for it and asked no questions, although I did wonder what a *bovina* was, as I knew the word referred to, of all things, cows.

I decided to try the gas station, since it was within walking distance, and to my surprise I found there a new *bovina* in a cardboard box. I took it back to the mechanic, who put it on and asked me to start the motor again.

"Now it will march well," he said with assurance. But when I started the motor, it missed and coughed exactly as it had done before.

"That settles it," Eileen said. "Let's try to get to Palenque. Maybe there is a better mechanic there."

I gave the frustrated mechanic five pesos for his effort, and tried to go forward. The motor would suddenly make a burst of speed. Then it would suddenly start hitting on one cylinder, and we would stop. Our progress was in jumps and starts and stops, but before long we were in the street that leads through the village, the same street that had always been there. I recognized it. It was the street in which high grass had been growing one hundred and thirty-three years before, according to John Lloyd Stephens, and also just twenty-three years before, when Lowelito and I had been there. It led right up to that church in which Lowelito and I had spent one rainy night. Now there was no grass at all. Instead, there were many automobiles and crowds of people and dust.

We limped up this street, jerking and stopping, until we reached a place at the side of the old church and directly across from the

Hotel Palenque. Of course there had not been any Hotel Palenque in 1950. Only one empty parking space was left, and we managed to cough into it.

People seemed to be everywhere, and among them we noticed a lot of long-haired North American young men and a few North American girls with hair hanging straight down their backs. We also noticed that many of the automobiles had U.S. license plates. This was certainly not the Palenque village of Stephens and Catherwood, of Graham Greene, or of Lowelito and me. The village of Palenque had become a place of tourists.

Nothing had changed in this village over a period of a hundred ten years, but during the next twenty-three years, changes were such as to make the place almost unrecognizable.

I looked across the street at what had been the abandoned roofless, floorless church, which in the past had stood on a grassy eminence connected to the grass-covered street. In 1840 Stephens had written that a boy could tumble out of the church onto the grass and roll on the grass down the street. No boy could do that now, for harsh stone steps led up to the level of the church and onto a scrubby garden in front of it.

A barrel-vaulted roof of solid concrete now straddled the old walls, creating an effect that was both ugly and cruel. As I looked at this structure, now no doubt a functional church, I had a great desire to free the walls of the heavy monster which had settled down upon them. Never had I imagined what the original roof might have been, but I could now see that even a thatched roof would be more pleasing to the eye than what was there. Nevertheless, I felt that the effect of this renovated church was in keeping with the spirit of the village as I now found it.

We unloaded our bags and Eileen's fragile wood roses and went into the hotel. We registered at a desk behind which sat a middle-aged Mexican man. We were directed to a room on the upper floor. This room opened onto a long balcony overlooking a backyard filled with trees, flowers, chickens, one burro, and a man building an adobe wall. On the street side of our room was a bathroom with a shower. The bathroom also contained a toilet, in which the water ran constantly. From the long balcony, onto which all the rooms of the upper floor opened, we had a view of the distant blue-green, jungle-covered mountains. I knew that the old Mayan ruined city was over there at the jungle entrance, looking just about the way it did when it was abandoned mysteriously eleven hundred years before.

Eileen came out of our room and joined me on the balcony, where I was sitting in a Mexican chair comparing the old Palenque village with the present one. "The first thing we had better do," she said, "is get that car running again. We won't even be able to get out to the ruins without it. Let's go look for a *real* mechanic."

We went down into the street where our Volkswagen was parked, and I began asking if there was a mechanic in town who understood Volkswagens. The first person I asked was a young mestizo who seemed fairly well dressed. He said he would go get a mechanic. Before I could discuss our difficulty with anyone else, this young mestizo had returned with another mestizo, who was said to be a *mecánico*.

He lifted the engine cover, and I climbed into the car and started it. This time it put on a good show, sputtering, coughing, and spitting, as though it were angry at the world. A crowd had gathered around us, and many of the people began to laugh at the way the car was acting. Now it was smoking and smelly.

The mechanic examined different parts of the motor and then announced that what we needed was a *regulador*. That word, I thought, must mean a "regulator," and I believed that this mechanic must be right.

The motor was still going, missing and sputtering in a most irregular way, when suddenly a very small boy — one of the dozens of interested bystanders — put his little hand down on the side of the motor and took hold of a wire hanging there. When he did that, the motor quit missing and began to run beautifully. Not only had he found the trouble; he had fixed it. He could not have been over eight years old.

The whole trouble had been caused by a loose wire bouncing off and on its terminal. The mechanic was now acting as though he himself were a genius, as though he had repaired the motor.

"For this complicated job," he said, "you owe me five pesos."

I was so pleased the car was fixed that I did not argue with him but gave him the five pesos. I did, however, make sure that he saw me give the little boy ten pesos.

Now we could turn our attention to the village. First of all, I wanted to see if I could find the place where Lowelito and I had eaten with the large Mexican family. Also, I wanted to see if I could find Don Ernesto's ranch house. I wanted to examine the church again, and I especially wanted to get a clear picture of this new Palenque village, which had settled down upon and swallowed the one that had been here twenty-three years before. Only then could I make a comparison between this new village and the former one.

By recalling the old Palenque street and looking at the present church, whose location had certainly not changed, I was able to imagine a straight line which would lead to the thatched house on stilts where Lowelito and I had eaten with the Mexican family. When my eye followed that line, I found that a bigger and sturdier house, with plastered walls, had swallowed up the one we had known. As I looked at this new, fat building, I could not help wondering what would be its own fate, and I also wondered how many replacements had occurred on that same spot since Stephens and Catherwood were here. In their day, houses would collapse from time to time and be replaced by others so similar that the looks of the village never changed much. But now it was obvious that different building materials had been introduced, materials that required different ways of thinking. Because there were so many more people now present, many of them must have migrated to Palenque from other places, bringing new ideas along with them. This was not the same Palenque I had known twenty-three years before, even though it had the same name and covered the same ground. I did not like it as well, but from the noise the present inhabitants were making — going into and out of stores, riding up and down the street and in front of the church in dusty automobiles, mingling with tourists — it seemed obvious that they liked this village.

Now I remembered a strange concrete monument I had seen some years before in a remote mountain village in western Honduras. There was nothing at all like that little monument anywhere else in the village. Nothing could have appeared more unrelated to its environment. A metal plaque was bolted into the cement, and on the plaque were words in English which said that the monument had been placed there to commemorate a gift to the village by the U.S. government during the administration of Franklin Delano Roosevelt. The gift had been a water project that our government apparently had financed in that remote place. As I pictured that monument in my mind, I found myself wishing that out in front of the place where Lowelito and I had eaten chicken and beans with all those Palenque Mexicans, I could erect a monument and inscribe on it these words: "In memory of the Former Palenque Village of John Lloyd Stephens, Frederick Catherwood, Lowelito, and me." I would not put the name of Graham Greene on my monument; he did not like Palenque one bit.

· · ·

When our misbehaving car was making so many people laugh in front of the Hotel Palenque, one American couple standing there did not laugh at all. When I saw this couple, I was not only delighted, but also convinced more than ever that Palenque was now a part of the wide, wide world. This couple had, in addition to a true appreciation of Mayan art, a professional reason for being in Palenque. The husband, Dr. Spencer Rogers, was the director of a museum of anthropology in California, and he had brought his charming wife along. Both of them were fairly small, so the four of us were able to squeeze into our Volkswagen.

On the outskirts of Palenque, as we approached the village, a narrow road led off to a motel on the left. That first night the four of us went there for dinner. On display in the motel were several low-relief copies, reduced in size, of sculptures at the Palenque ruins. They looked as though they had been made by a North American artist. I called Eileen to come and look at them.

"They're pretty good," she said.

"I think they are, too," I said, "but look at them carefully, for tomorrow we'll be seeing the ones these were copied from."

I did not believe that any person, especially a North American, could successfully copy the sculptures at Palenque, and I wanted Eileen to get a good look at these objects at the motel so that she could compare them with the originals. I thought that if she agreed with me, my theory would be validated.

One difficulty in copying Mayan sculptures comes from the fact that the Mayan quality of line is not restricted to those lines that are visible. The copyist reproduces only those lines which he can actually see. It might seem that if he reproduced the visible lines accurately, the result would give the same effect as the original. Not so. Only when the visible lines are experienced as effects of movement, which vary in speed as well as direction, can one be aware of Mayan line quality. When one sees visible lines as such movement, one finds the movement continuing along invisible lines beyond where the visible lines end. In addition, Mayan lines have spatial "overtones," just as the plucked string of a guitar has audible overtones. All these subtleties simply do not exist for anyone preoccupied with reproducing the lines he is seeing, especially if he is reproducing those lines in stone, the working of which must take so much of his attention away from everything else. In trying to reproduce Mayan sculpture, an artist might conceivably create a true work of art, but it would not be Mayan art. The only way to recreate Mayan sculpture, as visual quality, is to become an ancient Mayan Indian, and that, of course, is impossible.

I was now very eager to enter the old Mayan city of Palenque with Eileen. I knew, though, that I would have to watch her closely, because she was always inclined to climb up onto the highest possible place. She had done that on the Hieroglyphic Stairway at Copán, Honduras, and, having reached the top platform and looked down the steep steps about a hundred feet, had chosen to descend, one step at a time, sitting down.

The next morning, the four of us went down to the hotel restaurant early. We wanted to go out to the ruins as soon as possible but had to wait a long time in the restaurant for the help to remove tables, chairs, and divans that had been stacked up almost to the ceiling. An all-night dance had taken place the night before in an adjoining *sala,* and all the furniture of the *sala* had been put into the restaurant to make room for the dancing. For a while we were seated in a corner with chairs stacked high all around us. Fearing that the chairs might start falling down on us, I asked a young man wearing a white apron if he thought he could clear out that corner for us so that we could have breakfast and get out to the Palenque ruins.

"The cook has not yet arrived," he said, "and there are no eggs yet."

"But all these tables and chairs around us might fall down," I said.

"That is true, but I must speak with the manager."

I thought I would speak to the manager myself, so I went out to the hotel desk and found there the middle-aged man who had been present when we registered. I got to talking with him. I told him that I had been in Palenque twenty-three years before and that there were then only two automobiles in the village.

"When I was here before," I said, "I stayed with Don Ernesto Ratike. There was one jeep and one command car in the village, and they had not yet worn down the grass in the street. Each morning a boy would take me and my companion out to the ruins. In the late afternoon, he would come out for us in that jeep."

"Señor," the man said, with a happy smile on his face, "I am that boy who carried you to and from the ruins in that jeep twenty-three years ago, and I also helped your *compañero* and one French engineer find a place where rum could be purchased."

We both enjoyed remembering that earlier time, before Palenque had been opened up to the outside world. The manager then told the waiter to make a safe place in the restaurant for us. As soon as the cook and the eggs arrived and the room had been put in order, we had breakfast. Because there was not much choice, we all ordered *huevos rancheros*.

.   .   .

The picture of the old Mayan pyramids and temples of Palenque that I had been carrying in my mind was that first view Lowelito and I had each day as we approached on foot through the great trees of the jungle. The buildings were gray and silent in the early morning light. They seemed barely able to hold their own against all the vegetation around them. The spaces between the buildings were filled with bushes, tall weeds, and the dark-green orange trees planted years before by Frans Blom. The weather had been hot and humid when Lowelito and I were there. It was so uncomfortable in the open, outside the temples, that we never got to the Temple of the Cruz Enramada, which Lowelito named "the Gates to Paradise." It stood out, beckoning to us, against a lacy background of jungle trees that climbed the mountain behind. But we were content to look across the weed-filled courts to that temple from the cool interior of the Temple of the Sun. In 1950 Palenque had been a silent, abandoned city of stone in the mouth of a green jungle. There were no brilliant colors, no reds, blues, or yellows, anywhere. No other people were there. We had Palenque to ourselves.

Now I was returning to that old ruined city after twenty-three years. This time I was not in a jeep with Lowelito and a boy driver, bouncing over a narrow dirt road that wound through weeds and bushes to the dark jungle. I was in a Volkswagen with Eileen and an anthropologist and his wife — and I was the driver. We were moving smoothly over a paved road toward that same jungle, which we could see just ahead of us.

The paved road was now swinging us gracefully up a slight grade, and suddenly we were among the great trees with orchids in their crotches. I knew that at any instant we should reach the place where the gray buildings of Palenque would come into view. To my surprise, when we got to that spot there was an unexpected distraction. Stone circles had been constructed to form seats and picnic tables around some of the big trees left in a wide clearing. Many automobiles — most of which seemed to be old Mexican taxicabs — were parked in that area, and over on the extreme right of the clearing was a small stone office where visitors had to buy tickets before they would be permitted to walk into the ruins of Palenque.

As we got out of the car, I shook my head vigorously to rid my mind of this distraction. Then I looked ahead to find what I had been waiting eagerly to see, and there they were: the Temple of the Inscriptions, the Palace Group, and beyond, the Temple of the Sun. To my horror they were spotted with colors. Bright spots of blue, orange, white, yellow, red, and green were scattered up and down the pyramid steps wherever I looked.

The four of us walked forward, I not taking my eyes off those colored spots. Soon, however, I saw that they were moving, and then that they were people dressed in bright colors. They had come in those taxicabs we had seen parked at the entrance clearing. These people were American tourists, and the brightly colored, energetic ones who liked to climb pyramids were plump women in slacks. That all these tourists were here was a disappointment; I had wanted Eileen to have the experience of being in an abandoned jungle city that was still abandoned. Now, however, twelve hundred years after the Mayan people had deserted their city, it was alive again.

The spaces between the pyramids and buildings at Palenque were now completely free of weeds and bushes, all the growth having been tramped down by the tourists. The large court floor between the Temple of the Inscriptions and the Palace Group was packed down so hard that not a blade of grass grew there. Clean trails led off from that area to all the other courts. We could go easily to the Temple of the Cruz Enramada — Lowelito's "Gates to Paradise" — without worrying about *garrapachos* in the weeds. Frans Blom's orange trees growing along the trails had almost doubled in size.

We walked immediately to the Gates to Paradise, the Temple of the Foliated Cross. To see it from the entrance of the Temple of the Sun, as Lowelito and I had done, had been something worth remembering, but from that distance the low-relief sculpture inside did not even exist for us.

I now watched Eileen observe that famous example of classical Mayan sculpture. I felt sure she was thinking of those sandstone copies we had seen at the Palenque motel. She sat down on a block of stone slightly to the left of the panel, and from that position she could see the sunlight falling on both the edges and the enclosed surfaces of the sculpture, revealing them in sharp detail. As I watched her sitting there so relaxed, her steady gaze taking in the entire panel as a unit, I wished it were possible to see the sculpture through her eyes, for I knew that her response was determined altogether by the form of the sculpture and was completely free of preconceptions. Eileen knows how to see the form of things, both their color connections and their spatial relationships. She also can see as well as anyone else from the ordinary, practical point of view, through the lenses of acquired information, beliefs, prejudices, preferences, and dislikes.

I decided that I had better get busy making a drawing while my view of the sculpture was unobstructed, for I was quite sure some of those tourists would be coming along soon.

After I had worked an hour or so, Eileen looked at my drawing. "That's a lot better than a photograph," she commented, "but you were right: Nobody can draw these things."

I knew that she did not mean to find fault with my drawing. What she meant was that no artist of our time could get into his drawing of a piece of Mayan sculpture all that the Mayan sculptor had put into it.

I have often thought that Eileen's ability to see so well is just another example of her tendency to explore. When she looks at a work of art, she does not just absorb it; she explores it. However, she follows only those roads laid out for her by the artist. If there are any jolts along the way, she feels them. Now that she had looked at the panel of the Foliated Cross, and had explored it, she left the Temple of the Cruz Enramada.

"I think I'll go over and climb that Temple of the Inscriptions pyramid now," she said. Down the steps and trail she went, while I continued drawing.

"Just be darned careful, and don't fall down," I warned.

She had not been gone thirty minutes when a small boy came running up, gasping that *"la señora de usted dice que debe venir inmediatemente al Templo de los Inscripciones."* ("Your wife says that you should come to the Temple of the Inscriptions right away.") The way he delivered the message convinced me that I had better hurry, so I dropped everything and followed him.

Looking ahead, I could see Eileen coming down the other pyramid much too fast for safety, and remembering how she usually descended pyramids sitting down, I was alarmed. Before I could reach her, she was already down and running toward me. At the same time, I saw the anthropologist approaching us from another direction, walking unusually fast. When we came up to Eileen, I asked, "What happened? This boy said you wanted me. Did you go down the tunnel to the tomb?"

"You should have been there!" she exclaimed, still panting. "No, I didn't go into that hole. It was plugged up; nobody could go down."

"What do you mean, plugged up?"

"It was plugged up by a fat tourist woman. She got stuck in it."

"Oh, for heaven's sake," said the anthropologist.

"It was awful," Eileen continued. "I wanted Everardo to come because I remembered that he got that mule up out of the well in Baja."

It was now lunch time, so we found Helen, the anthropologist's wife, and went to where Lowelito and I used to swim in a clear pool. Unfortunately the trees had been cleared from around that once-sylvan pool; there was no longer any shade there. So we all went outside the entrance gate and ate our lunch sitting on one of the low stone circles that surrounded the jungle trees.

In the late afternoon, when we left the ruins, the automobiles were still parked at the entrance. Those people really seemed interested in the old Mayan city. Their guides must have been telling them excellent stories.

. . .

We departed ahead of the tourists because I had hoped to find Don Ernesto's ranch house. I felt sure I could find it if it was still standing, even though many of the trees that might have served to guide me there had been cut down. If I could show Eileen where Lowelito and I had lived, then she and I could devote the rest of our time to studying the sculpture in the ruins.

We parked the Volkswagen in front of the hotel, and soon the four of us started walking south along a street where formerly only a narrow pathway had been. Buildings with brightly painted plaster walls now lined the street where twenty-three years earlier thatched huts had stood. But a still greater surprise awaited me, for looking ahead and to the east, I saw something I had never seen before in Mexico or anywhere else: an entire city of silver houses lined up along three or four straight, parallel streets. This city, or village, had not been there the day before. I was sure of that. It had moved in and settled down in this orderly way while we were out at the ruins, and it looked as if it were there to stay forever, a bright, shiny, metallic addition to the town.

We now walked up one of the long streets between these newly arrived, streamlined American trailers and campers. They made up a "convoy," and we were told that they were all "self-contained." The leader of this group was in the convoy business. Every year he organized a different group of clients, with their campers and trailers. Then he led the caravan down into Mexico. Each year he traveled over the same roads and to the same points of interest. Palenque was on his list. I was interested to notice that the streets between the rows of campers were covered with deep grass, just the way the street in Palenque village had been before progress had come to it.

After we had reached the end of the street and had climbed to the top of the hill, we found on our left a big, primitive wooden gate, large enough, when opened, to allow a wide wagon to pass through. The gate had a big lock and chain on it, so we were forced to climb through the spaces between the gate planks. Noticing this wide gate, I remembered that the last time I was in Palenque I had not seen any wagons. I remembered thinking at the time that the people there seemed, like the ancient Mayan Indians, unaware of the usefulness of wheels. I had seen no vehicles on wheels other than the jeep and the command car. There might have been some wagons there, but if so I had not seen them.

As I left the gate, I noticed some deep tracks, or ruts, leading from the gate down the grassy hill in the direction of Don Ernesto's ranch house. The deep ruts could have been made only by heavy wagons, perhaps when the earth was muddy. By now the ruts were thickly lined with tough grass. The grass was growing on the sides, in the bottom, and on top of the ruts, covering them completely. Obviously no wagon had passed over this old road for a long, long time. The anthropologist didn't notice the ruts; his attention was caught by signs that indicated the passage of hundreds or even thousands of years. For me twenty-three years was proving to be a long time, long enough for so many changes to come to both the village and the ruins of Palenque.

At the foot of the grassy hill we came upon a creek. It was the one Don Ernesto had jumped into each morning before dawn, the one Lowelito and I had waded at times and later crossed on the back of Don Ernesto's old horse. Nearly all the jungle trees that

had formed a dark wooded area along both its sides were now gone, and the creek itself was dry. A little footbridge now led across the dry creek bed.

We crossed the bridge and walked a few yards more. Any second now Don Ernesto's house should come into view to the left and at the top of the next hill. I looked up.

"There it is!" I almost shouted. "It hasn't changed. It looks exactly the same. It's the only thing here that hasn't changed."

Seeing that old weatherbeaten house in the distance at the top of the hill, with great dark trees behind it, was so exciting for me

145

that I started walking much faster. Without intending to do so, I left Eileen and the Rogerses some distance behind me. They were seeing the same house, but their speed did not increase at all. For them, the house was without significance. They were seeing it "aesthetically," perhaps, while I was projecting into it all those former hot nights and even the excitement I had experienced in those former days, when wild parrots quarreled in the tree-tops and the old Mayan city was over there in the jungle all alone waiting for us.

As I approached the house, I could see a man standing in the yard in front of the porch. Near him was a large grapefruit tree filled with yellow fruit. When I came closer, I could make out the figure of a woman in a hammock hung between the porch columns. The sun was setting, and dusk was moving in.

The man turned out to be one of Don Ernesto's two sons. Don Ernesto had died some years before, and this son was now living in the old house. He and his brother had been away at school when Lowelito and I were there, so I told him of our two weeks' stay with his father. The woman in the hammock was his wife. Now they had two sons, both of whom were away at school. The same pattern of life in the old house was being repeated. Looking at the woman in the hammock, I hoped that she would be able to hold out and not die as Don Ernesto's wife had done. I also was wondering if this son who was now living there was as lonely for conversation as his father had been.

It was getting dark. Mosquitos and fireflies were out. We all bade Don Ernesto's son good-bye, and it seemed to me I was also telling myself good-bye. We started down the grassy hill to go back to Palenque village. When we were about two-thirds of the way to the creek, Don Ernesto's son called out to us, "Won't you come back and stay awhile? Maybe you would like to have some grapefruit to take along with you."

CHAPTER TEN

Baja California Sur

After the road had been paved the entire length of the Baja California Peninsula Eileen suggested that we drive over it. She said we should be ashamed of ourselves for not having driven all the way down before the pavement was in. I reminded her that, paved or unpaved, that would be a long road to drive over in our old, clumsy four-wheel-drive truck.

I told Don Roberto Thompson that we were thinking of going. Some time earlier, before the paved road had reached even as far as El Rosario, he and LaRue had bought a camper and driven all the way down the peninsula. Now, realizing that they had made the trip when the roads were awful, I was surprised at his response.

"We'll go with you!" he said. "When do we leave?"

Because we had camped with the Thompsons in many parts of Mexico, both on the mainland and in northern Baja, we were delighted that they would accompany us on this long trip. At first we thought we should drive straight down the peninsula, but then we changed our plans and decided to go down the mainland side of the Gulf of Cortés as far as Guaymas, where we could put our campers on a ferryboat and land in Baja at the gulf port of Santa Rosalía. The country from there south would be completely new to Eileen and me.

Arriving in Guaymas in the late afternoon, we learned that the ferryboat would not depart until the following morning. So we drove out to the end of a wharf a mile or so beyond the place where the ferryboat was docked. Out at the end was a large grain elevator that was gutted and twisted, making a weird effect against the sky. Later I learned that an accumulation of gas given off by the grain had caused the explosion. Everything was clean and flat out there on the smooth cement floor of the wharf. The wind was blowing hard. The rough waters of Guaymas Bay were on three sides of us. On every piling perched either a pelican or a sea gull. We felt lucky to have found such a nice camping place so close to the ferryboat.

Early the next morning, we drove back and lined up to get into the big ferryboat, the wide-open end of which reminded me of the gaping mouth of a monstrous shark. Already about a dozen cars and trucks had lined up ahead of us, and others were coming into the line behind. We were feeling lucky again, this time because we were near the head of the line. Just after I had gotten out of our truck and had gone over to talk with the Thompsons, though, a Mexican official came along and began ordering cars out of the line ahead of us, telling the drivers to go to the end of the line. He came to the Thompsons' big camper and ordered Don Roberto to follow the others to the rear. I supposed that he was distributing the vehicles with the intention of equalizing, or balancing, the load within the ferryboat. When he came to our camper, he stopped and read a little sign I had painted on the back door. The sign I had painted was "La Quinta Chilla," which can be translated as "The Poor Farm." La Quinta Chilla was also the name of the chickpea farm that belonged to Señor Álvaro Obregón before he became the president of Mexico. Our camper was not at all elegant. In fact there was something about it that made it look as though it might belong to a Mexican farmer.

After the official had read the sign, he saw me standing nearby and asked if that was my camper. When I said, "Sí, señor," he told me our camper should stay in line where it was. When we finally had crossed the gulf and it was time to drive the vehicles onto the shore at Santa Rosalía, I noticed that our camper was given priority over all the others. I had a feeling that either the ferryboat attendants felt sorry for us, or else they knew about that former chickpea farm of President Obregón. Our old, run-down-looking camper received favored treatment a number of times thereafter on that trip.

Don Roberto knew every detail of the country from Santa Rosalía on south; he and LaRue had struggled through its mud and dust and over its rocks when the roads were little more than trails. Now, after we had debarked from the ferryboat and spent some time exploring Santa Rosalía, Don Roberto suggested that we camp on the long embarcadero that extended far out from the town to form a little bay. He explained that he had been there before and could lead us.

"You follow me," he said. He took off along the bay in a northerly direction, driving over a narrow dirt road that led between several big, dingy-looking buildings made of lumber. He would turn abruptly around corners, so sharply that I would lose sight of him. Then he would reappear from behind another building. I saw that I would have to keep close to his camper or get lost. Finally we came out onto the embarcadero, which extended a couple of miles out into the gulf. Far out near the end, with water on both sides of us, was where we were to camp.

By the time I caught up with Don Roberto, he had arranged his camper crosswise on the embarcadero, let down the awning that he always carried rolled up on the side of his camper, unfolded some chairs and a table, and poured himself and LaRue a drink of rum.

"What a wonderful camping place this is!" Eileen said. "How did you ever find it?"

The place was so clean and so level, the sea breeze so cool, and the view across the bay to the town so pretty. It seemed too good to be true. The thought came to me that we should not be there, that soon some cop would come along and tell us to move. Hoping for the best, Eileen and I got out our own tables and chairs. We all settled down like a colony of squatters. It looked as though we were planning to make the place our permanent home. Eileen brought out her hors d'oeuvres. We were happy and relaxed.

The sun was setting deep red, a startling background for the white plumes of smoke rising from the chimneys of the old copper smelter across the bay. We sat there watching the sun gradually melt away until we realized that very soon the darkness would set in. Eileen and LaRue began setting the table and putting many good things on it for our supper, gourmet items they always brought along and stored in the campers in places only they knew about. When everything was ready we all sat down around the folding table. Don Roberto even brought out a bottle of wine. This being a happy event, it deserved to be celebrated properly.

"What a place to be camping," I was saying.

"Aren't we lucky!" came Eileen's echo. "Just look at that view across the bay."

At that moment I felt something scratching and pulling at my pants down by my left foot. At first, I thought it might be a sweater that had fallen from the back of a chair. But that thought was quickly dismissed, for now something was scratching and pulling at my other foot, and objects were running over my shoes. As I looked down, I heard Don Roberto exclaiming in a loud voice, "What the hell!" LaRue was screeching and Eileen was yelling, "Everardo!"

We were being attacked by big, gray-brown rats with beady eyes. Not by a dozen, but by hundreds of them. They were under our tables, they were climbing up the legs of the chairs, they were all over the ground, under our campers, everywhere. They were scurrying about. They were even trying to climb onto us. Clearly those big rats were not at all afraid of people; in fact, they were very friendly. They seemed overjoyed that we had come. Their movements showed that they were only begging for food, but they were so wild in their scampering, and so big and ugly, that we left the tables with everything on them, escaped into our campers, and slammed the doors. That was the end of our dinner party.

The next morning I saw Don Roberto open his camper door and peer out. The food we had left on the tables was all gone. But no rats were in sight. They had returned to their homes among the great boulders piled to form a breakwater all along the open gulf side of the embarcadero.

. . .

As we drove back into Santa Rosalía later that day, I had a strong feeling that the town should not be there, did not belong there. I felt that it was a disgraceful blot on the peninsula of Baja California, an example of what man can do when his only aim is to siphon from the land whatever can be turned into money. Santa Rosalía had the misfortune to be near a "natural resource," a deposit of copper. This natural resource had been smelled out by a French mining company, which, with the aid of native Mexican labor, had managed to create a mongrel French-Mexican town of unique ugliness. I now remembered some signs I had seen a few years before along the narrow paved peninsula highway, signs announcing that the highway was being built for the *desarrollo económico de Baja California* (economic development of Baja California). Those signs were erected, I thought, by the kind of people, always in authority, who take it for granted that bulldozed land is more desirable than nature undefiled. As we left Santa Rosalía, I said a prayer for Baja California.

Now our destination was that stretch of beach that extends across the southern end of the peninsula. But it was our full intention to try to see everything visible to the naked eye all along the way as well.

After leaving Santa Rosalía, we found that nature reasserted herself, rising again far above man's puny presence, even though his presence in some spots along the way south was far from invisible. The great flat surfaces of the silver gulf waters abutting the hard humps of burnt-orange-colored land created an effect unlike anything in the northern half of the peninsula. Yet there could be no doubt that what we were now seeing was an extension of the northern part. We would have known we were still in Baja even if we had been brought down here blindfolded. The space up around Colonia Guerrero is connected with the space below Santa Rosalía. One's attention moves out into both spaces in the same way. When I looked toward the west and saw the band of blue that was the Giganta Mountains, I felt sure that "Baja" must be up among their rugged canyons, too, and I knew that Eileen and I would have to go up there and see.

.   .   .

On our return from those white southern beaches, we stopped to camp along the embarcadero in Loreto, the town where the first Spanish mission in the Californias was established. The gulf at that point came abruptly against a low stone wall. (Eileen noticed that there were no big boulders present in which rats might have made their homes.) This wall was on the east side of the street. On the other side was a row of houses. We camped next to the wall, with Don Roberto's camper in front and ours on a line behind. The water's edge was only three feet away. Looking east, we had a view of the Sea of Cortés and of Isla del Carmen, which rose a short distance out from the shore. The water seemed crowded with fish, and the sky with pelicans. Those pelicans kept nose-diving into the schools of fish, to Eileen's great delight. She never seemed to tire of watching that show.

A dirt road led from the ancient town of Loreto up into the Giganta Mountains and on to the old mission of San Xavier. Don Roberto and LaRue agreed to wait on the shore of the gulf while Eileen and I went up and visited the mission, regardless of how long it might take us to get there and back. They had camped in the shade of the old building on that previous trip when the two of them were alone and the roads were so bad. They did not feel like going over those bad roads again, but they knew we had to go.

Eileen and I secured everything inside the camper because we expected the going to be rough and did not want our canned goods and provisions to get scattered over the camper floor. Then, early one clear morning, we departed for those distant blue mountains, which looked so gentle and inviting from afar.

Crossing the north-south highway just west of Loreto, we were barely out of sight of the turn-off when we found ourselves in the wild countryside. A smooth but faint dirt road wound its way up a wide draw between large boulders, scrubby brush, and a few scattered *palo blanco* trees. We were going along so easily that

I began to think we would get to the old mission before noon. We were traveling through a gray landscape in which the bushes and trees seemed to move aside just enough to let us through. Mystery was around every turn in the road (which is always true in a natural setting where there are no people). The *palo blanco* trees were becoming more numerous. With their white trunks and limbs, they were strangely attractive, seeming more like animals than plants.

Suddenly Eileen pointed over to the left and said, "Look at that white burro among those *palo blanco* trees! We should get a picture of him. Here's the camera; run get his photograph."

I stopped the car, jumped out, and with the camera walked toward the burro. He really did look pretty against the sandy soil among those little trees that were almost the same color as his hide. I wanted to get close to him, but the minute the burro saw me leave the car he began walking away. When I increased my speed, he increased his. If I walked faster, so did he. I could never get close enough for a photograph. After a few minutes he and I, still the same distance apart, were out of sight of the car. It was no use; that burro did not want his picture taken. I had to give up and go back to Eileen.

Soon we had entered a landscape of low hills. Then suddenly our road led into a canyon, which became narrower as we went along. We came to a small stream running across the road, on either side of which were large white boulders. Palm trees shaded the entire area. We stopped at that place for a few moments for no other reason than that it was beautiful.

When we left that cool, shady place, we began a steep climb. The road became narrower, giving us an idea of what it might be before long: steep, narrow, rough, and full of surprises. We arrived at a switchback on the edge of a steep drop-off; I had to back twice to get around it, and thereafter I was prepared mentally for whatever the road ahead might offer. Soon we were climbing along a one-way dirt road on the face of a cliff, high above the canyon floor, and then we came out onto a narrow plain. On one side was a tree-filled canyon. The trees seemed to be immense fig trees, a domesticated variety, not the wild kind. They filled the canyon so completely that I could not determine its depth. I could, however, hear water flowing beneath the trees, and the sound seemed to come from far below us.

The road went close by the edge of this tree-filled canyon for a short distance, and then both the road and the canyon made a right-angle turn. As we turned the corner, there appeared before us a group of adobe houses with thatched and red-tile roofs. The area around the buildings was crawling with goats — white, black, brown, and spotted. They all came running toward us, bleating as though to welcome us, each with a distinct voice. With so many goats, one might expect that all their sounds would blend into one. Not so; each is a solo performer, regardless of how many other goats are performing at the same time.

I stopped our truck and got out. Because it was surrounded by goats, I would have to take care not to run over some of them when we departed. Looking ahead, I noticed that the road continued on past a small blue chapel a few yards away, and thereafter along the edge of a cliff, at an extremely steep angle. As I stood there contemplating the steep road ahead, I heard Eileen talking to someone in Spanish. An old woman in a long black skirt and a bright red blouse had come out of one of the houses and was standing among the goats. There was so much noise from all the goats that I was surprised how clearly the old woman's voice stood out. Apparently, living in the midst of goat noise had taught her how to make her own voice heard.

"*Buenos días, señora,*" I greeted her. "You certainly have enough goats here in this beautiful spot."

"*Sí, señor,*" she said, smiling. "They are my constant and only companions, for it is seldom that people come along this road, and when they do they never stop. I live here alone with God and my goats."

"Señora," I continued, "the lady with me is my wife. We are going to visit the old Misión San Xavier. Can you tell me how far away it is and how bad the road is?"

"The road in places is *muy inclinado* [very steep]," she said, "yet the distance is not great. But, señor, permit me to ask you not to address me as 'señora'; I am a señorita and have been such all

my life. On this mountainside I remain a virgin, and I am the only person remaining of my family, which came here two hundred years ago. All my ancestors are buried near that chapel you see by the road. And I remain a señorita."

This old woman was very thin and wiry. In fact, she had the figure of a young girl, except that she was scrawny. I wondered what her diet could be, and I imagined that she must live mostly on goat's milk and figs. It seemed incredible to me that she would be able to butcher one of her goats now and then for food.

Eileen took some photographs of the old lady among her goats and asked if there were some way she could mail her some copies.

"Yes," the lady replied, "send them to Señora Muñoz in Loreto. It is my intention to go there next year, and she will give them to me when I arrive."

To begin the steep climb along the cliffside road beyond the chapel, I had to make a sharp turn where the climb began. As a result I was forced to begin the ascent with no momentum. My old Dodge Power Wagon was very powerful in low gear, and I did not believe it would be necessary to go into four-wheel drive. At the beginning the road did not appear so steep when seen from inside the truck cab. Soon, however, I began to wonder what was holding us back. Although the car was in low gear, I could not increase our speed, and the road ahead obviously was much steeper.

"You'll never get up this hill if you don't get going," Eileen was saying.

"I know it, but I'm already in low gear, and this is as fast as I can go."

"We'll never make it!"

The car was moving so slowly that I threw on the brakes and stopped. We would have to go into four-wheel drive. That meant getting out and turning the ends of the front-wheel axles with a wrench. We did not have "Warn" hubs, which are so easy to manipulate. I cannot remember the name of the hubs we had, but they always gave me trouble, and my knuckles usually were bleeding before I could get the front wheels engaged. It was always necessary to lunge the car backward and forward before the job could be done. Because Eileen could not turn the hubs, I knew I would have to get out and do it, but I wondered if she could sit inside, hold the brakes on, and make the truck lunge backward and forward. I was afraid that if I let her try it, the car, with her in it, surely would plunge down into the canyon.

Eileen saw the situation clearly. "Let me out," she said, "and I'll put a big rock behind the rear wheels."

If we could only get the car anchored so it would not roll backward, I could try to engage the front wheels. Eileen got out, found two big rocks, and put one behind each rear wheel. When she announced that they were in place, I released the footbrake to see if the rocks would hold. To my great disappointment, the truck rolled backward over the rocks as if they had not been there. I put on the brakes again, both hand and foot, and the truck stopped. Obviously, we were in a bad situation. I did not even dare to back down, so narrow was the road. I simply did not know what to do next, and Eileen was not offering any advice. Suddenly, though, she said, "Listen! A car is coming."

I realized that if a car came up from behind, it could never pass us and would have to help us before it could get up the hill. Soon it arrived, an old, beat-up truck that seemed perfectly capable of making the ascent. That must have been because it was so light. The truck was being driven by a Mexican who was eager to help. After I explained to him how to use the wrench and told him that I would try to make the car lunge while he turned the hubs, he did exactly as told and in no time at all we had a functioning four-wheel drive vehicle. Eileen got in beside me, and away we went up the steep hill. The old camper seemed eager to get on, lunging ahead so fast that I had to ease up on the accelerator.

When we reached the top of the hill, with the Mexican truck right behind us, I stopped to thank the driver. The day was quite warm, so I opened the camper and took from our refrigerator three cold bottles of beer.

A short distance ahead we were again driving through scraggly brush interspersed with *palo blanco* trees. The road now passed through deep white sand. Many ruts had been cut here and there as though former drivers had been searching for the easiest route to follow. Suddenly I saw a short pole that had been stuck into the white sand on the right side of the trail I was following. Someone had attached to the slanting pole a narrow, weatherbeaten board, and on the board was written in barely legible letters, "Comondú," with an arrow pointing toward a faint trail that led off to the right.

"Look, Eileen," I shouted, "there is the road to Comondú, that place we've always wanted to see!"

Eileen was as excited as I was. "Let's follow it!" she exclaimed.

"No," I said, "we must go on to San Xavier, and we are almost there, I feel sure. The Thompsons are waiting for us in Loreto, so we'll have to go to Comondú another day."

By two o'clock that same afternoon, when the sun was beating

down fiercely, we arrived in the long street that was the pueblo of San Xavier. A solid row of adobe houses lined each side of this long street, and across the far end of it stood a stone building so honest and dignified in form that we felt humble in its presence. The thought came to me that this one jewel of art was all that was needed in all of Baja California, that because it was there, although in this lonely place, no one should ever say that Baja California was a land without art. The fact that few people ever saw this old church could in no way make its powerful yet gentle existence less real or less important.

As we sat there gazing at the old church at the far end of the street, I kept wondering why it was having such a hypnotic effect upon us. Not a person was in sight. Apparently the heat of the day had driven all the people into their cool, thick-walled adobe houses. There was not an automobile parked along the street, not even a burro.

"Isn't it beautiful!" Eileen said. "The other old missions don't approach it. None of them has the same spirit. Why is that so?"

"It must be," I said, "that this old mission expresses visually only the pure intent of the Jesuits, only what they *wanted* to achieve in Baja, that none of the mishaps and bad side effects of their effort ever entered into its form. They say the road to hell is paved with good intentions, but some intentions must be sacred in their goodness and purity."

Eileen had another thought about it. "This old building," she said, "seems to tell us that human existence, despite all that is bad in it, is worthwhile after all. I wonder how long the building will last."

"I don't know, but it is already over two hundred years old. It is the only mission in Baja that remains exactly as it was built. Usually two hundred years seems a long time to me, but here, for some reason, it doesn't seem long. I guess this building will eventually either fall apart and go back into the earth, or be swallowed up and choked to death by man-made forms of a different spirit. Maybe the travel agents will advertise it until a paved road is built to bring tourists, and a hotel is erected here for them."

"I'm glad we came over those bad roads to see it," Eileen said. "We will never forget it."

We drove on down to the end of the street and parked in front of the old church. To the west and the north, the Baja mountains rose sharply against the sky, while the old stone building with its single bell tower stood alone, spotlighted by the sun.

As we approached the entrance to the church, I noticed the date 1751 above the arched doorway, and I supposed it was the date when the building was under construction. Only a few years later the Jesuits had to leave Baja, and their work was taken over by the Franciscan monks. But the work of the Jesuits will have to be respected as long as the old church stands.

When we stepped through the doorway, it was as though we had left the earth behind us. We entered a world of cool, shady space filled with invisible spirits. As our eyes gradually adjusted to the darkness, we became aware of great, silent, inanimate forms all around us, and out from among them emerged, as if by magic, an old white-haired man who seemed to be a native of that dark world. Without uttering a word he motioned for us to follow him up a winding stairway of worn stone blocks to the bell tower.

Arriving in the bell tower on the heels of the old man, we looked out through the open archways past the great hanging bells. Outside, in the brilliant sunlight, was that world we had left behind. There it was with all its familiar Baja California objects. Clearly we were not in it. We were in a time capsule with the old man. We were where time stands still.

I had a strange feeling that the old man had helped build this church, back in 1751.

"Señor," I said, "have you taken care of this old church for a long time?"

"*Por muchos años* (for many years)," he replied. After he had spoken, he stood motionless for a moment, as though he were gazing backward over all those years.

"Some time ago," I said, "two friends of ours came here in a big brown car with an idol's face painted on the front of it. They told us they camped alongside the church. Do you remember them?"

"*Sí, señor*," he replied. "The man spoke Spanish like a Roman, but he looked very much like *el padre Serra*."

"Do you mean padre Junípero?" I almost shouted. That settled it! "Eileen," I said in English, "do you remember how many times I have told you that my reason for going to Mexico has been to find the Mexican who shot me at the Battle of the Alamo? I am going to ask this old man if he fought with General Santa Anna. Maybe at last I have found the Mexican who shot me!"

"Don't ask him," Eileen insisted; "you might hurt his feelings. Besides, what if he is your man? We would have no reason to continue wandering in Mexico.

"We haven't even been to Comondú yet," she added.

It's a Long Road to Comondú was composed on a Compugraphic digital phototypesetter in ten point Palatino with two points of spacing between the lines. Palatino Italic was selected for display. The book was designed by Jim Billingsley, typeset by Metricomp, Inc., printed offset by Thomson-Shore, Inc., and bound by John H. Dekker & Sons. The paper on which the book is printed bears acid-free characteristics for an effective life of at least three hundred years.

TEXAS A&M UNIVERSITY PRESS : COLLEGE STATION